Property
D0053668

MASTER
of
CEREMONIES

MASTER

of

CEREMONIES

a memoir

JOEL GREY

with Rebecca Paley

FLATIRON
BOOKS
NEW YORK

Author's Note:
This is a true story, though some names and details have been changed.

MASTER OF CEREMONIES. Copyright © 2016 by Joel Grey. All rights reserved. Printed in the United States of America. For information, address Flatiron Books, 175 Fifth Avenue, New York, N.Y. 10010.

Frontispiece, p. ii: Joel David Katz, Cleveland Playhouse Theater, 1940

The photographic and illustrative credits beginning on p. 245 constitute a continuation of this copyright page.

www.flatironbooks.com

The Library of Congress Cataloging-in-Publication Data is available upon request.

ISBN 978-1-250-05723-5 (hardcover)
ISBN 978-1-250-05724-2 (e-book)

Our books may be purchased in bulk for promotional, educational, or business use. Please contact your local bookseller or the Macmillan Corporate and Premium Sales Department at (800) 221-7945, extension 5442, or by e-mail at MacmillanSpecialMarkets@macmillan.com.

First Edition: February 2016

10 9 8 7 6 5 4 3 2 1

For K. Elmo Lowe

MASTER
of
CEREMONIES

PROLOGUE

October 1966, New York City

The nightclub comedian mopped his sweaty forehead with a breast-pocket hanky one too many times—the linen as yellowed as the teeth in his desperate smile. Everything about this man—the sweat glistening through the pancake makeup; his thinning, dyed-red hair; the tasteless jokes that fell just short of his dropping his pants—was proof for the audience of how hard he was working for them. Men who were drunk and still drinking sat beside their rouged women on burgundy leather and gold button-tufted banquettes, everyone's head thrown back in overenthusiastic laughter. The spotlight on the small parquet dance floor that doubled as a stage was broken by the crossing of harried waiters trying to keep up with drink orders and the delivery of the roast beef special. The clatter of forks and knives against dishes competed with coughing from cigarette smoke and laughter . . .

I awoke soaking wet, wrung out from what was not just a disturbing dream but also a memory of a real event. I was now a thirty-eight-year-old man with a beautiful wife and two wonderful children I was able to support with an established career assembled from an eclectic mix of stage, screen, and TV work. The dream's vivid details, however,

catapulted me back a decade, to the early fifties, when I was still trying to make it.

I had been on the road back then with a nightclub act developed
around the idea that I was too young to be in a nightclub, let alone
perform in one. I was already in my early twenties, but I looked much
younger, because I was fresh-faced and, well, short. So I did songs such
as "Zip-a-Dee-Doo-Dah" and jokes such as describing current events
as "ancient history." Boy, did the audience roar at that one. I had been
worried that my naive material wouldn't work in the bawdy atmosphere
of the nightclub circuit. But in city after city, they ate it up. One of
the newspapers called me the "comic comet."

On my night off during a tour stop in St. Louis, I went to see a well-
known performer at another club. I had heard that he was the hottest
thing in town and wanted to know what the competition was up to. As
I sat watching the comedian in the loud, smoky room, the spotlight il-
luminating his aging face, I was stunned. His broad delivery employed
every virulent stereotype: take-my-wife jokes, fat jokes, crude sex jokes
(but not Jewish jokes, since the obviously Irish comic was playing to a
mostly Jewish crowd). When he did his fag impression, lisping and
mincing, in a bit about "fresh fruits," and not the kind you find in a
grocery store, I felt sick to my stomach. But it wasn't his crassness that
offended me most. It was his effectiveness. He would do, and did do,
anything for a laugh, battering the audience into loving him. I couldn't
believe that someone so willing to pander, someone who stooped to
the lowest levels of "entertainment," offering the most base and hack-
neyed material in exchange for the audience's affection, was actually
getting it. They were in his thrall, screaming with laughter.

Perhaps the crowd-pleasing entertainer onstage hit a little too close
to home. He was the epitome of everything I had been trying to escape ever since the moment I became an "overnight sensation" at the
age of sixteen after doing a wild song-and-dance act in my father's
variety show, *Borscht Capades*. I had first fallen in love with performing as a nine-year-old actor at the Cleveland Play House, one of the

country's best professional regional theaters. Although fame and financial success came to me first by working nightclubs, I never wavered from my desire to become a legit theater actor and return to that early, formative experience on the stage. I wasn't sure what it would take to make it in the theater, but despite the struggle that was all I ever really wanted.

And here it was. After more than fifteen years of struggling, I was finally about to fulfill that dream—to create my own role on Broadway. The subject matter of the show, *Cabaret*, was more than risky. And the emcee I would be playing didn't have a single line of dialogue. Still, it was full of possibilities, and it was mine.

I shook the image of the "Jerk of St. Louis" out of my head and pushed back the covers. It was deadly quiet in the apartment. The rest of my family had already gone off to their individual lives—my wife, Jo, to her morning yoga class, Jennifer to school across town, and James to the park with our housekeeper. I showered, shaved, dressed, and went into the kitchen for my espresso and toasted bialy. Then I started putting together my stuff for the day: script, dance shoes, an extra shirt, Sen-Sen, and a Hershey's Bar with almonds.

As I boarded the M10 bus in front of our apartment on 86th Street and began traveling down Central Park West, I felt slightly hungover—from the dream or anxiety about the show; I couldn't tell which. There were only a couple of weeks of rehearsal left before we were scheduled to open *Cabaret* in Boston for the out-of-town tryout before Broadway. I was still wrestling with my part, a fact I couldn't admit to anyone. I knew my songs and the choreography. And, thanks to the German icon Lotte Lenya, who was playing Fräulein Schneider, my accent was becoming quite convincing. Still, something important was missing—the man underneath the makeup.

The basic idea of my character was conjured from a master of ceremonies at a seedy club in Stuttgart where the show's director had been stationed in the Army. The director told me that this small man, who wore too much makeup, was bigger than life. But there were no specific notations or descriptions in the script regarding my character. It didn't specify his connection to the narrative of the show or even if he had a name. He was simply referred to by the abbreviated form of "master of ceremonies": Emcee. With five musical numbers that played in between the book scenes, yes, the Emcee was clearly a metaphor for the corruption of the Weimar Republic, which paved the way for the Nazis' rise to power. But go play a metaphor—not possible.

For the past four weeks, the ensemble, dancers, and I had been working long hours on John Kander and Fred Ebb's brilliant songs and Ron Field's edgy choreography in a big, cold dance studio ten blocks away from the George Abbott Theatre, where the director, Hal Prince, held the main rehearsal with the actors in the book scenes. Today, however, was the first run-through in which the cabaret numbers would be integrated with the book scenes. As the bus drew closer to the George Abbott, I found myself getting anxious. Everyone would see that I hadn't fully found my way as the Emcee. What had been passable in isolated rehearsals, as pure music and dance—showbiz numbers— wouldn't work when combined with the drama of the show.

I got off the bus at 54th Street and Seventh Avenue and walked two blocks east to the theater, where Hal, John, Fred, Ron, and the rest of the group were assembled. There were the principals, Jill Haworth, Bert Convy, Lotte Lenya, Peg Murray, Jack Gilford, and Edward Winter. There were the Kit Kat Girls, and there was me.

"Places, please, for 'Willkommen'!" the stage manager called.

As the cast went to their places in the wings, I nervously looked at Hal Prince, who was about to get off the stage and make his way into the house, where he would watch and take notes. Suddenly, I had an idea. I grabbed Hal and quietly said, "I have something I'd like to try."

"Fine," he said.

Silence.

Drumroll . . .

Cymbal crash . . .

Vamp.

Oom-pah-pah, oom-pah-pah
Oom-pah-pah-pah, oom-pah
Oom-pah-pah, oom-pah-pah
Oom-pah-pah-pah, oom-pah

. . . And there was I in the sweaty body of the comedian from my dream.

"Willkommen, bienvenue, welcome! Fremde, etranger, stranger . . ."

There he was; there was I; there we were. Everything that was a bit too much—overly friendly, leering, shocking, and in your face.

"Leave your troubles outside. In here it is beautiful. The girls are beautiful. Even the orchestra is beautiful."

And on comes the all-girl band, pushed by the Kit Kat waiters. This new, different Emcee had no compunction about manhandling the girls. Although I had no makeup and was wearing only a tailcoat over my rehearsal clothes, I became another person by fully discovering the inner life of this character. The change took the dancers and ensemble off guard. I could feel a bristling of discomfort as I lifted up a Kit Kat Girl's skirt with my cane and an intimidated resistance as I sat down on the lady piano player's lap. The choreography was the same, the same steps I had repeated many times in rehearsal, but the spirit in which they were done was mercenary, lascivious, and menacing.

I embraced everything that was in poor taste and not acceptable, and the ensemble responded in kind. They, too, were changed.

Near the end of the first number, the music pulled back to half time.

"Willkom-men! Bienvenue, welcome. Im Cabaret, au Cabaret, to Ca-Ba-Ret."

I sang the last words—seated on a chair lifted into the air by the waiters—as the stage manager yelled "Blackout!" and the sleazy comedian slipped away. Now just Joel Grey, I ran to the back of the stage, looking for an escape, all the while thinking, *You're a crazy person. Look what you just did. Say goodbye to a career. Nobody wants to pay good money to watch a creep.*

I had just shown the crème de la crème of the legitimate theater—that place I had wanted to be since forever—all that I had worked for years to rise above: the cheap tricks of the vaudevillian, the vulgar jokes among the musicians in my dad's orchestra, the fag impersonations of a sleazy nightclub comedian. All the things I didn't want to be.

Panicked and overwhelmed with shame, I tried to lose myself, hiding behind a flat at the back of the stage. I had one last horrible thought: *Everyone will think that is me.*

I felt a presence coming up behind me and turned around. It was Hal, who put his arm around my shoulder.

"Joely," he said, "that's it."

"You're just like me," she would say. "You're your mother's son." I was yet another reflection of how special she was, her prized possession for whom nothing was too good.

CHAPTER ONE

Great platters of food covered the table. There was herring, glistening pink with onions and swimming in sour cream; warm, homemade coffeecake; and sour pickles from the barrel. Chewy bagels and garlic-centered bialys and a seeded rye sliced thick and fat, dense pumpernickel. Big slabs of sweet butter, pot cheese, eggs, fruit (dried and fresh), everything top-of-the-line.

"Morris! You forgot the whitefish," my grandma Fanny said to my grandfather, who ran his own fruit-and-vegetable stall in Cleveland's Central Market. Having the pick of the produce, he always brought home perfect specimens of apples, pears, pineapples, cherries, or whatever was special and costly. Grandma Fanny wouldn't take anything less than top-drawer. Using elegant china and starched, white linen almost blue in its cleanliness, she arranged the bounty so that her table was as beautifully composed as a Brueghel painting.

That Grandpa Morris had a job in the first place during 1938 was not so easy, but selling produce was backbreaking work. He'd leave every morning at three o'clock to head downtown to the market where, in Cleveland's freezing cold or scorching heat, he'd lift and lug gigantic boxes of potatoes, cauliflower, and onions. Despite his punishing efforts for the benefit of the family, Grandpa Morris did not get a lot of sympathy from its members.

"War is everywhere, and your mother wants whitefish," he said.

"Sha!" Grandma snapped. "My soup is getting cold."

Life had never been simple for either of my grandparents, who had arrived in Cleveland as part of the great migration of Eastern European Jews fleeing pogroms and poverty. But the Depression and increasing anti-Semitism at home and abroad brought an uneasiness to the city's East Side, where most Jews, including my grandparents, lived.

If anyone could weather trouble, however, it was the Epstein clan. With their dukes-up hostility, they were one tough bunch—and the toughest of all was Grandma Fanny, née Borodofsky (changed later to Borad). A small woman with a strong presence, she made the long trip from Russia to Cleveland all alone at sixteen. In America, she found herself with no immediate family members or education, but Fanny was a fighter and raised five daughters with very little money and even less English. What a force she was. Even though she could barely read English, Fanny got a driver's license ("I gave da guy a couple bucks"), which she used to drive Grandpa's truck.

Fanny ladled out her signature barley soup, finishing each bowl with a large pat of butter that melted into the velvety, salt-and-pepper-speckled surface. With her hair cropped short in a no-nonsense style, she wasn't one to make a fuss over appearances. Her favorite accessory was the apron she always seemed to be wearing.

A natural in the kitchen, she was highly specific about how her food was prepared and consumed. And that included Sunday brunch, which was a non-negotiable event. Every week, all members of the family were expected for better or worse to sit and enjoy Grandma Fanny's fantastic spread, which was her singular form of mothering. No matter how tough times were or how cruelly they treated one another, as long as everyone was present and there was an abundance of food, Fanny felt the family was all right.

Sunday brunch at the Epsteins' was a kind of battlefield. My four aunts—Helen, Esther, Frieda (who called herself Fritzi), and baby Beverly (whom everyone called the "mistake" because she was born eight years after her older sister)—were always present. The Sisters, as they were known, took their mother's side against Grandpa Morris, who could do no right. Whether forgetting the whitefish or losing an entire day's pay in a pinochle game, there was always something to criticize.

If the weekly gathering at Grandma and Grandpa's brick house on Grantwood Avenue was a combat zone, then Mother was its biggest offensive. Sitting next to her, my baby brother, Ronnie, and my dad at the big dining room table, I could see The Sisters jealously appraising the charming dress and matching coat Mom had sewn for herself from a Vogue pattern. Wherever she was, my mother, a small, dark beauty, always made sure all eyes were on her.

Everywhere we went, the butcher, the baker, the grocer, people fussed over her not only because she was so pretty but also flirtatious and eager to be seen. At the market, I noticed how the owner, Mr. Friedman, would look her up and down while personally fulfilling her request for large pearl tapioca. She made the most of her feminine powers and charm, but it wasn't just men who found Mother appealing. She also had tons of friends, like Bea Sandson, who looked up to her, copying her daring style and recipes. The phone never seemed to stop ringing in our house, and it was always for Mother.

My mom's charisma was just one aspect to the trouble between her and The Sisters. There was also the matter of Grandpa Morris. The man her sisters considered a bum was nothing short of a prince to my mother, and she was naturally his favorite. A very tight pair, both were olive-skinned, attractive, and always pulled-together (at the table Grandpa wore a snappy bow tie, white linen shirt, and pleated trousers as if he were a Southern gentleman rather than a Midwestern fruiterer). They both also loved gambling (Grandpa played pinochle and poker; Mother and her circle played mah-jongg) and dancing. She was her father's daughter, Grandpa would say to Mother, which galled not only The Sisters but also Fanny. Their criticisms only strengthened the bond between my grandfather and mother, and they frequently defended each other to the rest of the family. Case in point:

"Why are you wearing a tie," Grandma Fanny said to Grandpa Morris. "It's brunch."

"Leave him alone, Ma," my mother responded sharply to her mother before training her big, lovely smile on her father. "I think he looks very handsome."

The Sisters pounced on my mother in retaliation. Ronnie and I put our heads so close to our soup bowls that we nearly dove in.

"What? You didn't have enough money to add buttons?" said Fritzi about my mother's swing coat. "How do you close the thing?"

My aunts snickered, but Mother was undeterred.

"There isn't meant to be a fastening. It's the *style*. I made it from the same pattern Carole Lombard wore in *Fools for Scandal*."

"Listen to her," Aunt Fritzi said, shaking her fork in my mother's direction. "Now she thinks she's a blonde movie star!"

My aunts never held back their hostility toward the sister they had nicknamed the *Schwarze Jabbe* ("black frog"), because she had darker skin than the rest of them. Instead, they laughed at her expense over their barley soup. In the open war between my mother and her sisters, each side gave as good as it got. (When Aunt Fritzi was on her deathbed, suffering from emphysema and barely able to talk, lying there ashen and frail, she beckoned me to come closer. I thought she intended to kiss or embrace me, but instead she whispered in my ear, "I always hated your mother.")

Mom acted like she couldn't have cared less what her sisters thought about her. At home she called them "classless" and "vulgar." My mother's ambitions went way beyond them.

She was the only one in the family who changed her name, going from Goldie to the more American Grace Anita when she was twelve years old. (When Grace didn't suffice in her remaking, she changed the spelling to Grayce.) After she appeared in a few school plays, she started to dream of a career as an actress—and even entertained the idea she might end up in the movies. Like so many other young girls at the end of the 1920s, she loved the new, exciting medium of the "talkies." Mother saw herself up on that big screen while watching Mary Pickford play a melodramatic flapper in *Coquette* or Ruth Chatterton as the mother of an illegitimate child in Lionel Barrymore's *Madame X.*

But her deadly practical family thought she was out of her mind. No matter how beautiful she was, according to everyone except her adoring father, Morris, Goldie would never be in pictures. Grandma accused her of *faygelech in bosom*: "fluttering birds in her breasts," or unrealistic dreams. By the time Mother became a wife and the mother of two sons, the only remnant of her acting fantasy was her singing "Papirosen" around the house. While preparing a pot roast for supper or rearranging the tchotchkes she so carefully accumulated, she warbled the lyrics of the popular Yiddish song about a poor orphaned immigrant girl, dressed as a boy, selling cigarettes and matches on the street.

Kupitye koyft zhe, koyft zhe papirosen.
Please, please buy my cigarettes.

Still, she continued to see herself as someone special. She took after her mother's hardworking ways only in the effort she put into reinventing herself. Mother took great care and a lot of time every day with her hair, makeup, and clothing—taking her cues from the latest styles of movie stars and magazine models. She was resourceful, making beautiful outfits with very little money, proud to look like a wealthy woman even though she was far from one.

The most glamorous choice my mother made, however, was the man with whom she had fallen in love and married. Meir Myron Katz, better known to the public as Mickey, was something of a minor celebrity as a clarinet and alto sax player in Cleveland's biggest music

halls and popular nightclubs. Mickey couldn't have been more different from the plodding fellows her sisters had married, such as Irv, the
kindly husband of Helen (the eldest), who ran a candy store; or the
deadly practical Eddie, who ran a grocery business with his wife,
Esther. Although Mother adored her father, Mickey was in a different
sphere from him as well. Yes, they were both incredibly hardworking,
but my father got applause and adulation for his work. Sure, our family
didn't have any more money or live too far from the rest of the Epsteins
on Cleveland's East Side, but Grace had married an *artist*. To her mind
that made us inherently better.

In some ways my father's family wasn't too different from Mother's.
They also had emigrated from Russia with little to nothing, but the
Katzes were a far gentler bunch than the Epsteins. My grandfather
Max, well known in the community as Mendel the tailor, had
brought my grandmother Johanna to America after their marriage had
been arranged by a broker in Latvia, where he had stopped on his way
to the New World. Johanna was an educated woman who spoke several languages, while Max had had no schooling whatsoever. But together they navigated a life in the new land that was Cleveland, which
offered its own share of hardship. I remember my dad telling me that
one of his earliest memories was of standing by his father's side outside
a hospital, where his mother was suffering from a breakdown after losing an infant child, and wondering when or if she was coming home.

My father eventually had three siblings: his brother, Uncle Abie,
and two sisters, Jeannie and Estelle. Despite financial struggles, all the
children somehow received music lessons. Abie played the violin, Jeannie the piano, and Estelle danced ballet en pointe and sang. The family held concerts at home on Saturday nights, which they called *Katz's
Follies*. On summer evenings, neighbors would gather on the street outside their apartment to listen to the music coming through the open
windows.

Dad was the serious musician in the family, even something of a
prodigy. With his small pencil mustache, pomaded side-part hairstyle,

and fine features, he looked like a performer (although not a Jewish one—there was nothing the least bit Semitic about his appearance). As a teenager he played clarinet and saxophone in the high school band and picked up small jobs around town doing the same. He and his baby sister, Stell, entered every amateur night they could find, but not as a brother-sister act. Pretending not to know each other, each gave an individual performance, doubling their chances of winning the grand cash prize. "Myron Katz" played a version of "The Saint Louis Blues" that brought the house down, while "Estelle Kay," a perfect doll in her hand-sewn ballet costume, melted the audience's hearts with her song and dance routine en pointe. Often, it was a tie between the two of them, and Dad and Stellie would split the prize, which they would turn over to Johanna for much-needed grocery money.

At fifteen, Dad became a professional musician. He joined the Musicians' Union and was a regular with the Johnston Society Orchestras, playing everything from stag parties to country clubs. Although he continued to attend high school until he graduated, my father became the major breadwinner in his family. He supplemented his own father's meager income and supported his brother through college so that Abie could become a pharmacist.

Right out of high school, Dad was hired to go on the road with Phil Spitalny (one of the talented Spitalny brothers, who both were composers and orchestra leaders from Cleveland). It was while waiting at the train station to leave for the tour that my seventeen-year-old dad met and fell instantly in love with my mother ("The most beautiful thing I'd ever seen in my life," he said). She was fourteen, and after they married, two years later, they were hardly ever apart again.

By the time I was born—and Ronnie, four years later—Dad had become a fixture in the Cleveland music scene. As a kid, I loved to tag along with Dad to the RKO Palace Theatre, where he played in the orchestra under the direction of Maurice Spitalny, Phil's brother, who was well known for the tight white flannel pants he wore to show off his "manhood" while conducting. There was no more magnificent destination than the vaudeville theater and picture house. You couldn't get any grander than the two sweeping staircases of white marble, imported crystal chandeliers, and hand-woven, 67-foot gray carpet adorned with roses. And that was just the lobby! The gigantic, 2,800-seat theater with its vaulted ceilings of painted friezes and gold leaf could have been a real palace. It was nice enough for the famous comedians George Burns and Gracie Allen to get married there.

I never saw the show from the audience, but I couldn't have cared less. As far as I was concerned, the view from the orchestra pit underneath the stage was the best one in the house. Hidden off to the side, I kept true to my promise to be quiet and not "get in the way" of stagehands, wardrobe people, performers, and anyone else running around. There was no way I would have ever misbehaved—I just so loved being there. (That's why Ronnie wasn't allowed to go; he was too little to be quiet.) I watched the supporting acts come onstage, which could be as many as ten in a night. There were magicians such as Ade Duval, who could make a cocktail shaker disappear and brought scarves to life in his "Rhapsody in Silk" act, and dancers such as Toy & Wing, formerly of the tap-dancing trio the Three Mahjongs, who were dubbed "the Chinese Fred Astaire & Ginger Rogers." I marveled at the pageant of comics, animal trainers, opera singers, mentalists, and more, all introduced one after the other by big, electrically operated name cards, just as they were in nearly every vaudeville house across the country.

The bright lights were always changing, changing, changing as I tried to see what was going on and who was doing what. When the card would flip to the name of the famous headliner—Jean Harlow, Edith Piaf, Sophie Tucker, Jack Benny, Milton Berle—the excitement and applause would rise to a delicious crescendo. It was something I wanted to be a part of, although I didn't know why or how.

I loved being around Dad when he was at work. He was not only a virtuosic clarinetist, but I could tell that his fellow musicians absolutely adored him. Whether it was the other players in the RKO orchestra;

the members of the big band he used to play with at the Golden Pheasant Chinese restaurant; or the klezmer musicians with whom he did bar mitzvahs and weddings, they all wanted to hang around him, because he had a story for everyone.

My father made it his business to listen to and collect stories during the week. He'd regale the other musicians with them while they were changing into their tuxes in the dressing room or were tuning up in the pit. My father's repertoire—which came from comedy acts, the music store where he bought his reeds, or even our family—fit perfectly into the scene. Everyone crowded around him, laughing at his jokes and praising his musicianship. My father's stories were hilarious but never vulgar or mean; that just wasn't his style. Dad was a very sympathetic person, the kind of guy who always stuck up for the underdog or tried to help when there was a problem. Once, while playing on the steamer *Goodtime,* a pleasure boat that went from Cleveland to Put-in-Bay, he witnessed a black couple being told they were not allowed to dance. His response was to stop the band. "If they can't dance, then I'm not playing," he said.

The admiration and affection my father received from his bandmates and countless audience members each night differed vastly from the lack of respect he got at home. Mother, who believed her station in life was elevated because she had married a creative type, was ambitious for him and found the sound of his clarinet as vibrant and soulful as anyone else. And my father worked hard—three or four jobs a day, seven days a week—to be a serious provider in a tough field for a family man. Yet behind closed doors, she chastised him for a litany of flaws that included his thinning hair, paunch, and inability to buy a house. She even criticized him for his personal pleasures, such as smoking cigars.

"Do you have to smoke that awful cigar in the house?" she said.

"Sweetheart, you know I love my ACs," he said, referring to his preferred brand of Antonio Y Cleopatra cigars.

"You're getting the ashes all over. And it stinks."

"Grace . . ."

"And pull up your pants. Your stomach's hanging out."

She was following Grandma Fanny's example of cruelty, although Mom would have been mortified at the suggestion. My mother, hardly an analytical type, was completely unaware that she was treating Dad exactly as her mother had treated her own father—and so was I. As she picked on every one of his vulnerabilities, including those over which he had no control, such as his bad stomach, I watched and worried.

Dinner was a particularly worrying time of the day. Mother, who lavished the same attention, time, and skill on the food she prepared that she did on her appearance, was an exceptional cook. The menu for the wonderful dinners we sat down to every single night could include anything and everything. But it was always a many-course meal: roast beef with Lyonnaise potatoes, steamed asparagus with hollandaise sauce, and apple pie for dessert. *The Settlement Cook Book* was her bible, and she devoured its recipes for meat, salads, puddings, and cakes. But she was also adventurous and of-the-moment in her culinary efforts (there was never a discussion of our keeping kosher, since neither of my parents had grown up in strict kosher households). If there were a new recipe in the paper—Waldorf salad or curried lamb—she was the first to try it. Besides her looks and sense of style, Mother's cooking was a big part of her appeal, all the more proof of just how very special she was.

But when my father's stomach was upset, which it often was, and he couldn't eat a bite of what she made, Mother acted as if it were a personal attack.

"But Mickey, you have no idea how good this is, and how hard I worked on it," she said as we quietly dug into a soufflé while my father had white rice with a little cinnamon and sugar, or plain toast.

The way my mother treated my father—who always took it, barely fighting back and never blowing up—made Ronnie and me even more upset. But I was caught between disapproving of her meanness and needing her approval. The more she laid into my father, the more it seemed I was safe from her castigations. So I often took her side. *She's right*, I'd think. *Dad's a slob.* But not without guilt for betraying him.

I also acted like my mother by splitting my dad into two men: the brilliant musician who was honored and beloved at the Palace, and the henpecked man at home who allowed my mom to treat him poorly. Throughout their entire relationship, Mother always loved to watch Dad perform. That never changed. She admired his talent, but she also craved the attention that she received when she went to see my dad at places such as the Alpine Village supper club, where people came up to her to say how wonderful her husband was.

So, although I knew I wanted to be a performer, like my dad, and loved to watch him when he was working as much as my mother did, I definitely didn't want to be a musician. I rebelled against the piano lessons I was given, which was fine with Mother.

"You're your mother's son," she would say. "You're just like me."

She claimed me for herself by saying that we had the same temperament, taste, and talent. I was yet another reflection of how wonderful she was, her prized possession for whom nothing was too good. She had named me after her favorite leading man, the handsome movie star Joel McCrea. Mother always made sure I was impeccably dressed and my hair was perfectly combed. It was her habit to dress me so that I caught people's attention just as she did.

In the outfits my mother made for me (in one photo, I am in a white sailor suit with a tiny gold band around my little three-year-old ring finger—I never found out what that ring was about), I definitely got noticed. Being watched was not an unusual phenomenon for me. My first memory of what it meant to capture a crowd's attention begins when I was six, performing the duty of ring bearer at the wedding of my father's baby sister, Estelle. As I walked down the aisle carrying the ring on a small pillow, everybody oohed and aahed at my perfect white satin tail suit.

Even at home I commanded an audience—albeit one not as willing.

Ronnie was constantly being shushed by Mother while I played the perfect son. She dressed up Ronnie, too. With his olive skin, almond eyes, and dark hair, he was gorgeous and looked more like her than I did. Still, he was more of a set piece, while I had the speaking part.

"Ronnie, be quiet; your brother is singing."

"Ronnie, please, your brother is explaining what the teacher told him."

When her girlfriends would come over to play mah-jongg, or "mahj," as they called it, Mom would introduce me, her talented son, and I would do everything but curtsy. Meanwhile, my brother, who had learned not to talk so much, sat in his chair like a lox. I seemed to be the most important thing in her life, certainly more than my baby brother and maybe even more than my dad.

A family story had it that I was born with that something special. According to the tale told by my father's side of the family, I was just three weeks old, with everyone hovering around the bassinet, staring down at me, when I raised my arms and spread my fingers in the unique fashion of the Kohanim blessing a congregation. My grandfather and father, both well-known members of these descendants of the high priests of ancient Israel, agreed that it signaled I was someone for whom they could have big expectations.

If in the house of my father's parents I was a blessing, in that of my mother's family I was a deadly troublemaker. The Epsteins had their own story about me they liked to repeat over and over. It went like this:

When my mother was giving birth to me, she had terrible difficulties. After sixteen hours of excruciating labor, the obstetrician entered the waiting room to report to my father and Grandma Fanny that the baby's head was too large to get through the birth canal. It looked like only one of us would survive.

"Who should we save?" the doctor asked. "The mother or the baby?"

My father fainted, but Fanny answered without hesitation: "Save de tree. There'll be more branches."

Luckily the doctor's prognosis turned out to be wrong, but The Sisters never let me forget how I had almost killed my mother. No matter how many times my aunts told and retold the story of my birth, it never lost its ability to wound. Particularly since my mother, who always listened to the story without comment, never stopped her sisters from telling it. She never protected me, just as, I would bet, her mother didn't protect her. Shame was the Epsteins' way—they shamed my mother for thinking she was better and having a different nature. ("Who does she think she is?") And they shamed me for the pain I caused Mother.

I thought that The Sisters were right about me—that I was bad. What else could explain Mother's terrible moods, which came and went unexpectedly? Ronnie and I never knew how long they might last—maybe hours, maybe a day—but her displeasure was always announced the same way, with a low, off-key humming through clenched teeth. She often chose the haunting melody from "Summertime." But sometimes I would hear her humming and half-singing the plaintive Yiddish song "Vos geven iz geven iz nito."

"What was, was, and is no more."

And then you'd better not talk to her.

The same mother who meticulously dressed me in starched shorts and a matching collared shirt with a little gold ring; who made my favorite chocolate cake with six layers of creamy frosting; who told me I was *hers*: This same woman wouldn't even look at me. Stiff-armed, she would stare out the kitchen window at cold Cleveland, humming her mournful tunes.

Being shunned by the most important person in my life was painful, but the alternative was even worse. If she wasn't glum, she was wrathful.

"Get over here," she'd say, but we knew better.

That guttural timbre of her voice, that low tone, was her introduction to rage. It was a sound that she saved for only these moments.

When we heard the flip in her voice, we would make a run for it. Unlike my father, neither of us would willingly step forward for punishment. Instead, we would bolt down the long hallway of our apartment and dive under our beds, screaming, "No, please!" Then it was chaos. She'd come after us with a broom, jabbing it furiously under the bed to route us out, yelling, "You bad children . . . bad . . . How did I end up with such brats!"

The bristles hurt when they hit my arms and legs, but that was nothing compared with the beating I knew I would receive if I surrendered.

"Get out from under there!"

I never understood what we could have done to make her so angry. I was always so careful. *Always.* But it had to be something. Maybe we didn't clean up the dishes when we were supposed to, or we didn't wash them well enough. Or maybe we spilled something on the sofa. Whatever it was, I knew I deserved it—just as my father deserved her ridicule for being who he was.

After a time, the broom would retreat and so would Mother. Still, I would wait before coming out from under the bed to make sure that it was safe. When it was and my mother's mood had passed, I would return to my role of the perfect son.

My first leading role, as a young pilgrim climbing a very tall watchtower, was a true test of my mettle as an actor. I was petrified climbing the flimsy ten-foot set piece, but the audience didn't know, because I climbed as if I weren't afraid.

CHAPTER TWO

The school bus dropped me off at 105th Street, from where I surveyed all the trees, grass, and ponds of Rockefeller Park below. A ten-minute walk and I was home. As soon as I entered the large and stately lobby of the Sovereign Hotel, I was boiling. Even though it was a 50-degree Cleveland spring day, Mother, worried I would catch a cold, had overdressed me as always. I took off my hat and plaid, cold-weather jacket, put them down next to my lunch box on a big burgundy leather chair, and went over to the reception desk.

We had moved to the large residential hotel two years earlier, when I was eight years old. It was still only ten minutes by streetcar from Grandma Fanny's house, but according to Mom we were stepping up in the world. There were maids that would come to clean our apartment every day, ballrooms where they held wedding parties on the weekend, and a concierge desk manned by Larry.

Standing in front of a wall of hanging keys and messages in little cubbies, the old man wearing a mustache, glasses, and Sovereign uniform was easily annoyed by my questions.

"Hello, Larry, are my parents upstairs?"

"No, your mom and dad are out."

When Dad wasn't out at or traveling for a job, he was sleeping late after one. I usually saw him only when I got to tag along to the RKO or on outings to Uncle Abie's nearby drugstore, where I loved standing among the tight, tall aisles packed with bottles, jams, jellies, and tubes of mysterious purpose. Mom, too, was often out, either off playing mah-jongg with her girlfriends or shopping for unusual ingredients to make a new recipe.

"Where's my brother? Is my brother up there?"

"The babysitter is up there."

Uh-huh. Effie and Ronnie. I'd rather be alone. No matter how old my little brother grew, to me he was just a baby.

I asked Larry if Susie Kovach, one of the few children in the hotel, was home. She and I went to different elementary schools, and I had assumed that was because she was an immigrant. She and her mother had moved to Cleveland from Prague not long before we moved into the hotel.

When Larry replied that he didn't know, I said, "Could you call up please and ask Mrs. Kovach if Susie is there?"

Annoyed, he picked up the house phone.

"Mr. Joel Katz from 10B is downstairs and wants to know if he can come up . . . You can go right up."

Mrs. Kovach, a nice lady with a thick accent, opened the door. With her somber clothing and worried expression, she was so different from my own mother. But sometimes she gave Susie and me finger paints with a funny smell that I loved to use. She showed me into the living room, where Susie was already doing her homework. After Mrs. Kovach left to get us a snack, Susie leveled her serious blue eyes at me. Under her straight blonde bangs, they made quite an impression.

"Mama can't get in touch with Teta Ingrid," she whispered. "She's very upset since we probably shan't see her again because of what is happening to the Jews."

This wasn't the first time Susie had brought up this subject. She often talked about how she and her mother, who had escaped Prague, were afraid for the family they had left back there.

In this way, Susie filled in some of the information my parents had tried to shield Ronnie and me from. Although they tried to whisper or speak in Yiddish (Dad was fluent), I knew 1942 was a time of terrible things for the Jews in Europe. I overheard stuff such as Dad's phone call with Uncle Abie about the Jewish passengers of the transatlantic liner *St. Louis*. They had been forced to return to Europe, and their story was all over the news.

"President Roosevelt is letting those boats go back?" my father said in a tone that was both concerned and questioning. "How can that be? He's been so much on the side of the Jews . . . Do you think the papers are right? I read they sailed so close to Florida they could see Miami's lights . . . It's a *shanda*. Women, children. Jews. All those people are going to be killed."

Killed?

Why would anyone want to kill Jews? I was Jewish—why would they want to kill me? Was there something wrong with us?

Roosevelt was a god and a great president—so Dad said—but if he couldn't protect the Jews, who could? My father's phone call left an indelible mark as did so much else about being Jewish at that time. There was a deep-seated anxiety about the goyim. Being Jewish was dangerous—in Europe at the moment but anywhere eventually. Even collecting money to plant trees in Israel, a perennial Hebrew school project, made me uneasy. I wondered as donations dropped into those little blue boxes whether one day we would have to leave the Sovereign and move there.

After finishing my homework and the snack with which Mrs. Kovach had returned, I looked up at the clock on the wall and saw that it was nearly 4:00 P.M. Jerry would soon be starting his shift. I quickly gathered my things, said goodbye to Susie, thanked Mrs. Kovach, and headed to the elevator.

Elevators in buildings were still rare, and the fact that we had one where we lived made the place seem exciting and luxurious. The decor of the Sovereign's elevator—dark wood paneled with shiny brass, a hand-operated lever, and soft overhead lighting—confirmed its importance. But the real thrill for me was Jerry, the pale-skinned, sixteen-year-old bellboy who ran the elevator every day after he finished school.

Sometimes he let me work the elevator, which I loved to do, but the best part of being with Jerry was that he treated me like an equal. Even though we were six years apart, he took an interest in me and shared things about himself: from a big, Irish family who lived in the poor west side of town, he hoped to go to college on a baseball scholarship. When he described the Cleveland Indians games he went to, I pretended I was interested (if someone tossed a baseball to me underhanded I would find a way to injure myself catching it). I loved talking to Jerry no matter what the subject—sports, homework, even the girls who walked through the hotel lobby.

"She's pretty, isn't she?" he said after a cute blonde girl visiting one of the guests went by.

"Did you see that one?" he said about a sexy redhead. "Now, *she's* gorgeous."

"Yeah. She really is something. Do you go out with her?" I might ask.

That's how it began between us, with girls, with how men are *supposed* to talk until one day the talk about the sexiness of girls shifted into something else.

"You know something, that's making me horny," Jerry said while discussing a buxom, older woman who lived on the fifth floor. "I'm getting hard."

Silence.

"So am I."

He stopped the elevator between floors and slipped his arm around my shoulder. I thought to myself, *What are you doing?* I didn't speak. I smelled dry-cleaning fluid on his uniform.

When the buzzing for service became frantic, he returned his hand to the lever, put the elevator back in motion to pick someone up. I went along for the ride, hands folded in front of me, like any ordinary passenger.

From the moment Jerry dropped me off at my floor—the elevator doors closing on his smiling face—until his next shift, I couldn't wait to see him again. To ride up and down in the elevator, talking about homework and the hotel. To feel the thrill in my stomach at his touch.

Jerry's affections solidified feelings and impulses within myself that I had trouble naming before we began fooling around. When we first met, I was immediately attracted to him, even though I didn't understand it as such. Months before our first encounter, I couldn't take my eyes off him and would find any reason to take a ride in the elevator. Afterward, the whole thing seemed so obvious. He was handsome and strong, and we liked each other. Yet when I was off the elevator, I was keenly aware we weren't supposed to be doing what we were doing.

I explained away the unnerving early stirrings of my sexuality with a member of the same sex by using the closeness—acceptable within the confines of the playfulness of boys—that I shared with my cousin Burton. The only child of my mother's oldest sister, the dour Aunt Helen, and her harried husband, Irving, Burton was born a month before me and was roughly the same height. But that's where the similarities ended. From the small apartment where he lived above his parents' candy store on the west side, Burton did all the normal things a ten-year-old boy was supposed to do—at least according to the Epsteins. He played sports and wore regular clothes, unlike me. My best sport was jumping rope with the girls (I wasn't allowed to play anything too rough for fear that I might get hurt).

We adored each other because of our differences, not in spite of them. I admired him for his conventional clothes, strength, and position as Grandma Fanny's favorite, the only child of her firstborn. In turn, he thought that I was something glamorous with my artistic family and flair. We cared for each other a lot, so alone in the quiet of Burton's bedroom, cuddling under the covers, we felt comfortable to explore normal urges that for us started at about nine years old. The erotic aspect of our closeness was innocent and exploratory—the normal stuff of kids. But we also sensed that if our family found out what we were up to in his bedroom, they would not be happy. Outside of the cocoon of Burton's bedroom and Jerry's elevator, boys weren't supposed to be like that with boys. It felt right to me, but I knew it would get me into big trouble.

I was taunted by the neighborhood bullies for much less. When my mother dressed me in a green bow tie for picture day at school, she said, "You look wonderful!" But on the way to the school bus the boys on the corner shouted, "Look at the sissy!" It was ironic my mother chose outfits that made the kids call me queer, since she was no fan of the faygelehs (the Yiddish word that meant little birds was derogatory slang for the flittery-fluttery outcasts with lisps and limp wrists). When my parents would have friends over for cocktails and start to get a little loose, I would overhear them making fun of any musicians who seemed a little too swishy.

Although I felt safe in Burton and Jerry's embrace, out in the world, the disgust in the voices of my parents, their friends, and the kids on the block alerted me to a very real danger. Their insults posed a threat against which I had to be constantly vigilant. I had to protect myself from *queer* or faygeleh being leveled at me. I had to conceal the closeness and comfort I had with certain boys.

It sometimes felt as if danger lurked around every corner of my childhood—my mother's erratic, angry moods; the murderous hatred of the Jews that Susie Kovach described; my feelings for boys that would make everyone else hate me. There was even a period of worry in the house about my being so small, as if I were freakish. Mother looked into pituitary shots, but that didn't go anywhere, and I remained forever in the front row for my class pictures. The result of all this anxiety was a permanent state of hyperalertness for being born who I was (small, sissy, Jewish). I always kept my antennae up for signs of trouble. A boy looking at me a beat too long or a group of more than four of them congregating on the corner was reason to turn and go the other way.

There was, however, one place where it seemed as though nothing bad could happen, a safe haven where I was free to let go of my caution.

From the moment I first walked into the Cleveland Play House, when I was nine years old, a feeling of pure joy washed over me. Mother brought me on a special date (Ronnie had to stay home with Effie the babysitter) to a Saturday-matinee performance by the Curtain Pullers, the children's program, and I was enchanted as we walked into the Drury Theatre, the bigger of the two that made up the Play House's complex on Euclid Avenue. I had never been to the theater, and as soon as I got there I knew I was *someplace*.

The refined stone and masonry work gave way to the 560-seat apron-stage theater, which had been converted from a church. As I nestled into the seat beside my mother, I thought about how the theater's beauty was so different from the calculated glamour of the RKO Palace Theatre, where my father played in the orchestra. The Play House didn't dazzle; it impressed. Its patrons, too, were different; they looked as if they were in a real church (or what I imagined people looked like in church). The adults holding playbills, the boys in gray flannel pants and blue blazers, and the girls in smocked dresses were all refined and serious. A respectful hush filled the theater.

Then the lights went down and the performance began. I didn't know what the play was or who the Curtain Pullers were—but as I watched the children up there in their colorful costumes telling us a magical story, I pointed to the stage and whispered to my mother, "I want to do *that*."

Mother enrolled me as soon as the performance ended, and the following Saturday I joined the dozen or so other Curtain Pullers in the drama class taught by the very severe Esther Mullin, who made it clear from the onset that one had to measure up no matter how insignificant the exercise. She didn't have a lot of humor, and she told it like it was. The way she nailed people for bad acting was scary, but I could also see what she meant when she talked. Recognizing the art Miss Mullin was instilling in us, I not only feared but respected her.

Even when it was my turn to be criticized, I didn't mind so much, because I was learning something new and important.

"Is *that* supposed to be walking through a door?" she said to me one day in class. "You're just *showing* something; you're not really *doing* it. Make me see the door. Now, go again."

Miss Mullin was right, and I worked on doing it the proper way, walking through that door so everyone could see it!

I loved class and being in front of an audience that had paid 25 cents a seat to watch my fellow miniature thespians and me in our weekly plays. My first leading role, as a young pilgrim climbing a watchtower to warn the populace of a dreadful storm in *Hurricane Island*, was a true test of my mettle as an actor. It wasn't my lines or the complexity of the character's emotional state that proved challenging, but rather the daunting task of climbing a very tall ladder to reach the platform where I was supposed to wave frantically to the other pilgrims (offstage). I was petrified climbing the flimsy ten-foot set piece, but the audience didn't know that, because I climbed as if I weren't afraid. *As if* nothing bothered me. *As if* I were brave and strong. That was the job, so that's what I did.

Hurricane Island, a real confidence booster, was an early, very crucial lesson in performance—not just onstage but also in real life. Learning to do things "as if" was a discovery that turned out to be an invaluable tool as an actor and as a person with secrets. I adopted a confident stride, different from my own, so that no one on the street would finger me as a sissy. That walk became so ingrained that I no longer remembered what my own true way of walking was.

I acted in a wide variety of children's plays and parts from the title role in *Jack of Tarts,* to the wicked wolf in *Little Red Riding Hood,* to Little Black Sambo in a musicalized version of the classic children's story in which a "Topsy" wig transformed my blond curls into cornrows tied up with little colored ribbons and makeup turned my white face black (not the Curtain Pullers' finest moment). Through the much-needed framework of the Play House, I began to gain an identity—and a reputation.

After the artistic director of the Play House, K. Elmo Lowe, saw me in one of the Curtain Puller rehearsals, he asked Miss Mullin if she thought I could handle a part on the main stage. She said yes, and soon I was auditioning for the part of eight-year-old Pud in the Play House's production of Paul Osborn's Broadway smash hit *On Borrowed Time.*

For my audition, Mother dressed me up in high-top boots, a plaid mackinaw jacket, and the Daniel Boone coonskin hat that was all the rage with the under-twelve set. When I arrived for my meeting with Mr. Lowe looking as if I had got lost hunting rabbits, it was all he could do to stifle his laughter. Calling to his wife in the greenroom upstairs, he said, "Miss Paxton, you've got to see this."

Walking behind Mr. Lowe into the room where the actors hung out between rehearsals and performances, I was keenly aware of the photographs of previous Play House productions that covered the walls. Serious young men and dreamy women stared out at me as I readied myself for a chance at a place in one of those pictures on the wall.

"Mrs. Katz, would you mind waiting downstairs," Mr. Lowe said, breaking me out of my reverie. I looked at my mother, who, having followed Mr. Lowe and me into the greenroom, appeared just as startled as I was.

"Thank you very much," he added, and Mother left the room.

It wasn't hard to understand how he had been a matinee idol back in the 1920s (legend had it that in his early years at the Play House, the theater couldn't hang his picture in the lobby because it kept getting stolen by love-struck women). With his thick crop of pushed-back black hair, natty tweed jacket, and six-foot-four frame, K. Lowe was the epitome of highbrow glamour.

He had joined the Play House in 1921 when Frederic McConnell—his classmate from the Carnegie Institute of Technology Drama School, in Pittsburgh—became its managing director. Together they brought national recognition to the amateur company, and it was now the nation's oldest resident professional theater. Although Mr. Lowe continued to act as a member of the company, he had also become a renowned director who had influenced the careers of many successful Play House alumni.

I took off my coonskin cap and my jacket and began my audition. The material from *On Borrowed Time*, a dark comedy about Death in the form of a man named Mr. Brink who comes for my character's parents in the very first scene, was heady stuff for a nine-year-old. By the second scene Mr. Brink has come for Granny. Then it's Pud's grandfather's turn, but Gramps tricks Death by trapping him in a tree so that Mr. Brink can't take him away from Pud, who has lost everyone. The only problem is that as long as Gramps doesn't die, no one else in the world can, either.

When I finished with the line "Don't want my whole life ahead of me. I want to go with you. I love you, Gramps," Mr. Lowe looked at me like I had just said something he had never heard before. He paused for a beat and then asked gently, "What would you do if your grandfather said, 'I can't be with you anymore. I have to go with Mr. Brink'? How would you feel if he would abandon you like that?"

"I would feel very sad and mad, too, mad that he would leave me. You don't love me anymore."

"And what would that mean, 'You don't love me anymore'?"

"Who is going to keep care of me? I would be sad and angry."

"That's right. Let's do the scene again."

After I had done it, he said, "That was very good, and you're a very good actor, Mr. Katz."

As I tried to do what he asked, I felt something new coming out of me, something he had drawn out of me, that I hadn't known I'd had. I put old feelings and experiences of my own short life into the scene. I thought about the deepest fear a kid can have—losing your mother. It made me angry and sad and scared all at once. And with that, the part was mine, and I stepped into the magical world of the Play House.

The weeks leading up to opening night of the play changed my life. First of all, I was allowed to go to school late, so that I could spend the mornings rehearsing. How I loved those mornings! Unlike the chaos and noise of school and home, there was such dignity and structure to the theater. At the Play House there were clear rules for behavior, and I was enthralled by the exceptional actors' manners. In accordance with British tradition, all the actors were referred to by their last names and the appropriate titles before them. That included me. "Mr. Katz, come to the stage, please."

The formality signaled to me that this was a serious art, of which I had the privilege to take part. No one in his wildest dreams would randomly change the playwright's words. There were no excuses for not having learned one's lines. Pride in craft was simply too high for that kind of amateur-hour stuff.

Although I was only nine years old and the Play House was the premier regional repertory theater, drawing tremendous talent from all over the country, I was treated as an equal. In the dressing room, veterans such as Johnny Rowe, who played Gramps, taught me the art of putting on makeup. I sat in front of the mirrors and bright lights, breathing in the spirit gum as the highly regarded actor turned into a painter, applying shading and lines to his face.

Showing up at the theater on time, learning my lines quickly, and remaining quiet when other actors were working, I was admired for my discipline and my naturalness. Even Esther Mullin, who was also in the production, respected me. (Esther played the villain of the piece, the terrible Aunt Demetria Riffle, who pretended she wanted to take care of Pud but just wanted the money—a real bitch *and* a great part.)

By the time I made my stage debut on opening night of *On Borrowed Time*, I fully understood the necessity of serious preparation, and the need for very hard work to create a successful theatrical production. As a result, I was prepared. I knew my lines and blocking. But I was *not* prepared for the weeping in the first and second rows! The 150-seat Brooks Theatre was filled to capacity. I heard audience members sobbing and blowing their noses during the last scene of the play—as Pud, having fallen from the tree and broken his back, lies helpless and in pain in Gramps's arms. "Take him, Mr. Brink. Take him now. Take us both," Gramps said. I stood up, smiling beatifically after all that pain, because my character had been carried to heaven and reborn— and so was I.

During the curtain call, holding hands with the seven other actors, a family, and having won the affection of the audience because I did a good job, I thought, *I want my life to always be like this.*

After the show, people clambered around me to say how my performance moved them. "It was so powerful." "How did you know how to do that?" "How could a kid so young understand all those deep feelings?"

Praise for my performance extended to the local press. "As for Joel Katz' playing of 'Pud,' I only can say that the boy is phenomenal," read the review of *On Borrowed Time* in the highly regarded *Cleveland Press*. "He is as completely at home on the stage without being the slightest degree precocious as any child I have ever seen." My first review was better than I could have ever hoped for! (Who knew that it wouldn't always be the case?)

But perhaps my biggest fan of all was Mother. She just loved the recognition I was receiving for my work onstage. If she used her husband's success as a musician to boost her self-esteem and standing in the community, imagine what it would mean if her son became a star. I was her flesh and blood, so if I were admired, it was in large part thanks to her. The dream that had burned too brightly in her youthful imagination had been magically rekindled. I was to be famous in her place.

My mother's pride in me had real perks. I relished her attention during the run of *On Borrowed Time*, particularly our late-night suppers at Wong's after the show. I felt so grown-up rolling into the Chinese restaurant at ten o'clock with my mother as if we were on a date. She ordered all my favorites: shrimp chow mein, sweet and sour pork, egg foo young. The food, even those disgusting cardboard fortune cookies, was a prize for giving a good performance.

I was in *On Borrowed Time* for months, then another play immediately afterward. I continued to get part after part, never wearying of the performance or rehearsal schedule. I didn't perform with the Curtain Pullers any longer, but I didn't miss it. Nowhere was I more content than at the Play House. I found every nook and cranny of the theater fascinating. While I was in a production of *Family Portrait*, being performed in the Drury Theatre, *Invitation to Murder* was being performed in the other small theater, the Brooks (where *On Borrowed Time* had been). When I wasn't onstage, I would go underneath the theater and wait below the other stage for the actress to lift the arm of her chair, causing a trapdoor to open. Night after night, she would drop straight down a hole in the stage, and I would be waiting below. It never got old.

One night, my father and mother each thought the other one was picking me up after a performance—so no one came to get me. Locked in the theater alone, I wasn't the least bit frightened. It was a dream come true! Onstage, illuminated only by a single ghost light, I recited to an imaginary, yet deeply enthralled audience the Queen Mab monologue from *Romeo and Juliet*, which Mr. Lowe had encouraged me to learn.

> *O then, I see Queen Mab hath been with you.*
> *She is the fairies' midwife, and she comes*
> *In shape no bigger than an agate stone*

I wandered up and down the steps of the four-story building, in heaven, trying on all sorts of costumes in the wardrobe department and practicing my entrance onto the stage. I would have been totally thrilled to sleep there, but, alas, my father finally arrived to retrieve me. Almost in tears, he had absolutely no idea how happy I'd been.

There was a lot that my parents didn't understand about the Play House. The Epsteins and the Katzes frequented Cleveland's thriving Yiddish theater. They often went to the Duchess and Globe theaters, owned by a furrier who produced Yiddish plays during the warmer months, when fur sales were slow. Many famous Jewish performers appeared there, such as Molly Picon and a young Paul Muni (born Frederich Meier Weisenfreund). But the legitimate theater was not the world of my family—certainly not my grandparents, who lived an almost entirely Jewish existence.

My grandfather Max, a passionate opera-lover, always listened to the broadcast from the Metropolitan Opera on the radio, even while he helped me prepare for my bar mitzvah. Sitting next to him in his tailor shop at 74th Street and Cedar in the middle of winter—the windows fogged up from the steam-presser, an egg salad sandwich my mother had made for us to share resting on the display case—I was practicing my maftir when he stopped me. I hadn't made a mistake in the recitation of my Torah portion. Rather, a recording of the late Enrico Caruso, one of my grandfather's favorite singers, was playing on the radio.

"You know," Grandpa Max said to me with his customary seriousness, "Caruzeh vas a Jew."

In Mendel the Tailor's worldview, everybody worthy of respect was Jewish—even the great Italian tenor. And who was going to deny it?

I, however, knew the difference between Gentiles and Jews—and there were definitely no Jews at the Play House. Except for one: Benny Letter, the head of construction and a fan of my father's, kept an eye out for me, occasionally inviting me to share coffee cake during his break.

"How do you like it?" Benny asked about the Play House.

"I love everything about it."

"That's good . . . And I'm here, too."

It was a reminder that Benny and I were indeed a little different from everyone else in the company. But I wasn't afraid of that difference. The fact that I was appreciated, even admired, at the Play House relieved some of my Jewish wariness of the Gentiles. How could I be afraid in such an inviting and pleasant place?

Mr. Lowe and his wife, Dorothy, were certainly as different from Grace and Mickey Katz as one could imagine, and in my mind for the better. I loved visiting the tall, handsome, and urbane Mr. Lowe and the fine actress and Southern beauty Miss Paxton in their special dressing room for two. The storied duo were the Alfred Lunt and Lynn Fontanne of Cleveland, often appearing together onstage, sometimes even as husband and wife.

They shared a professional life as well as a personal one, but that was not what distinguished them most from my parents. Mr. Lowe and Miss Paxton were educated, having both graduated from Carnegie's drama department, where they met. They were polite and soft-spoken, not just with others but also—astonishingly—with each other. I didn't know that kind of respect and gentleness existed between married people.

Because I came from a house where expressions of love were coupled with hostility, discovering a man and woman who respected each other in love and work, who were careful with each other, was a revelation. The relationship between Mr. Lowe and Miss Paxton couldn't have been *that* perfect, but to me, it was.

Hoping one day to have a marriage like theirs, I turned Mr. Lowe and Miss Paxton into role models and surrogate parents. In her honeyed Southern accent, Miss Paxton would invite me to join them for dinner along with their two daughters, P.K. and Stanja. She listened to my stories about home and school, accompanying my tales with her hiccup of a laugh, and met all of my odd little quirks—such as the green bow tie I continued to wear or my becoming overly dramatic when re-telling my day at school—with motherly affection. Miss Paxton, a real Southern belle, didn't have moods, only maternal protectiveness.

Mr. Lowe also showed concern for my well-being—often by keeping Mother on a short leash. While watching me grow as an actor, he intuited that her motives behind her extreme desire for my success had more to do with her than with me. Elegantly, he protected me, asking her not to direct me in my lines or telling her I would be fine at the theater for the day and that she could go. He was able to succeed at what few had before him: putting Mother in her place. To her credit, she accepted it from Mr. Lowe.

Still, I had an uneasy feeling of guilt that by loving Mr. Lowe and Miss Paxton as much as I did, I was somehow dishonoring my parents. Caught in a confusion of allegiance, I was torn between wanting to be safe and heard and wanting to please my mother and make her proud of me. While I knew my dad's love was a constant, something I didn't have to work at and could take for granted, my mother's affection seemed entirely conditional.

Above all else, I loved being with my mother, particularly when I could have her all to myself. So when she told me we were going to New York City, just the two of us, the prospect was over-the-top exciting. The purpose was to audition for the role of one of the sons in *Life With Father*. Based on a beloved book series, the heartwarming Broadway hit concerned a nineteenth-century Wall Street broker and his attempts to keep order at home with four lively sons.

Word had gone around the Play House that the Broadway hit production was looking to replace one of the sons, and Mom thought we should go for it. The plan was haphazard. Details on where this audition was to take place, or who had set it up in the first place, were sort of vague. But the biggest question I had was how I could play one of the boys, since they were all redheads. "Please!" she said. "If you get the part, they can dye your hair."

Mother took me out of school, just as she had for rehearsal at the

Play House, and we arrived at Cleveland's Terminal Station all dressed up for our train to the Big City.

The train trip, while exciting and romantic, was nothing compared with arriving in the city that was the epicenter of the American theater. In the cab from Penn Station to our hotel, we sped through block after block of theaters, the marquees rising, blinking, and calling out:

BY JUPITER STARRING RAY BOLGER

GERTRUDE LAWRENCE IN MOSS HART'S *LADY IN THE DARK*

GEORGE GERSHWIN'S *PORGY AND BESS*

CANADA LEE IN *NATIVE SON*

I had never seen so many people on one street! There were crowds of people, smiling, talking, smoking, pushing. There were policemen on horses and guys selling hot dogs and pretzels. Street musicians competed with honking car horns.

Having arrived at 47th Street, we made our way into the Edison Hotel, the biggest, fanciest hotel I could ever imagine. The Sovereign, where we still lived, was grand, but the Edison was truly glamorous. The Art Deco lobby was just as chaotic as the street outside. Bellhops dashed in between men in suits and women in cinched cocktail dresses with lots of jewelry. New York was everything I had imagined—larger than life, full of possibilities, and fast. It was also overwhelming.

At some point, I turned and suddenly realized that my mother was gone. I looked frantically around the lobby. Where was she? Barely a moment had passed since she had been right next to me. Then I spotted her, just a few yards away, talking to some strange man. She was smiling, her mascaraed eyes glowing so that even I knew she was flirting.

A few minutes passed before Mother called me over and introduced me to the handsome, older man. I was confused, but Mother quickly moved us along. "Joel, dear," she said. "I have the key. Let's go to the room." She said goodbye to the man, and we left.

Up in the room, the two of us changed for an early dinner in one of the hotel's exotic restaurants. As if in a romantic scene from the movies, I ate my strawberry flambé and listened to this beautiful woman across the table telling me what a good actor I was and how my talent would take me far. By the time the check arrived, I was ready to go back to the room to rest up for my audition and a day in the city.

Back in our room, I couldn't get over the sea of lights that shone below the window where I sat. I was so enchanted that I almost didn't notice that my mother was changing her outfit again, this time into a tight-fitting dress.

"Why are you changing clothes?" I asked. No answer. She continued to apply her lipstick and to fool with her hair.

"Where are you going? It's late."

"I'm going dancing," she finally replied. "There's a famous place around the corner called the Havana Madrid. It's a hot spot for Latin dancing."

"Am I coming with you?"

"Children are not allowed."

"You can't . . ." I started to protest.

"Sweetheart, you know your mother loves to dance."

"Are you going with that man in the lobby?"

"Yes, dear. But I promise you: One dance, and I will be back."

"Mommy. You *can't* go."

"It is late, but you can stay up for a little while. I love you, dear."

And then she was gone.

I was alone in a hotel room in New York City. I got so cold, I began to shiver. Then came the tears. Although I was considered mature for my age and spent a lot of time back home around adults or by myself, I was still just a kid. Left alone in a big and strange city such as New York was the scariest thing in the world. I looked out the window; I looked at the clock; I turned the radio on and off and on; I put more lights on around the room. Nothing helped. A series of terrible what-ifs raced through my mind. What if he was a bad man? What if he hurt her? What if she never came back? It was two o'clock in the morning when she returned. She came over to embrace me and I smelled alcohol on her breath.

"Why are you crying?" she said. "Mother's here."

"I hate you."

There never was an audition during that trip. We were supposed to call somebody, or somebody was supposed to give somebody else a letter, but "somebody" never panned out. I don't know what happened, and frankly I didn't care. Mother tried to explain, but I was not interested. The only lasting impression of the trip was Mother's volatility. Even if she said I was the greatest, "the sun, the moon, and the stars," that couldn't guard me from her unpredictability.

So it became clear: The only truly safe place for me was the theater. Over the next two years the Play House provided a harbor from the chaos of my mother, a place where I never found myself knocked between being wonderful one minute and bad the next, as I did during the Epsteins' Sunday brunches. In the acting company, I found a family of an entirely different sort. Here, you could say and feel whatever was inside you. Problems were solved and decisions were made by listening to different points of view. There was an exchange of ideas, because no one way would satisfy.

Difference celebrated, contradictions used as creative fodder: The theater was a collective endeavor in which everybody had his or her part to play. The company was made up of so many types—so many ages, body types, personalities, and talents. Some had children; others didn't. Some were married and some single. There were even men who loved men.

At twelve years old I already understood that Viktor and Bryan, two members of the Play House, were different. It was nothing I talked about with anybody, but still, I got it. They would leave the theater together and they owned a dog, a dachshund named Liesl. The snippets of conversation I overheard between them sounded just the way other couples talked. ("I took Liesl for a walk" or "Don't forget to pick up milk for the house.")

I didn't know exactly how or why, but I felt the stirrings of kinship in the unspoken intimacies of these two gentleman. I was captivated by the notion of our similarity. It's exciting when you recognize in others something in yourself that you didn't even know was a part of you. And it wasn't just about the kind of sexual connection I had experienced with Jerry, the bellboy. Viktor and Bryan were two men somehow sharing a life, a foreign but comforting concept. At the same time, the discovery that I identified with them frightened me. Everything I had heard up until now was that men who loved men were fairies, homos, limp-wristed perverts, sissies, and fags.

But Viktor was a very masculine leading man whom women swooned over. The discrepancy was confusing. None of those ugly words would make any sense in a sentence about Viktor. No way. Nor did they apply to Walter, another actor at the theater.

My relationship with Walter began when the two of us were cast in the same play. The theater is a very sexy place. It always has been and always will be. To inhabit another character, another presence, and another way of thinking, it is necessary to forget who you are. You strip yourself bare to give room to imagination. So you put whatever thoughts you have about yourself aside to become a killer, a philanderer, a genius—*anything*. The space to act out your dreams is arousing. That's why a lot of people have affairs with other cast members. With the line between pretend and real blurred, permission is freely given.

Walter and I had both been cast in a production of, funnily enough, *Kiss and Tell*. In the family comedy by the popular playwright F. Hugh Herbert I was Raymond, the bratty younger brother, and Mr. Lowe was my father. (How nice was that?) Walter played Dexter, the boyfriend of my onstage sister. Because of our ages—I was twelve and he was sixteen—we bonded immediately.

Walter came from the poorer West Side, where my cousin Burton also lived. His family of Croatian immigrants, who spoke no English, spent night and day making ends meet at their butcher shop, where their sons were also expected to work. Often Walter arrived at rehearsal with his hair smelling of garlic from having stuffed sausages all night. On breaks, we played cards, raced each other to the corner deli, teased each other—little, quick Joel ducking around tall and gangly Walter. Our camaraderie didn't arouse any suspicion because we were just the youngsters of the play. Why wouldn't we hang out together? Why wouldn't we be pals?

So when I asked my parents if I could sleep over at Walter's house, they weren't the least bit suspicious. By then, my family had moved to a house in University Heights, a suburb of Cleveland. Although it meant leaving the Sovereign, and Jerry, whom I never saw again, it was yet another upwardly mobile step for our family. It was also kind of far for me to travel home after dinner at Walter's house, which was the perfect reason for a sleepover. Not that I really needed an excuse with my folks. They trusted me to be on my own. ("You don't need to worry about Joel. He knows how to take care of himself.") If Walter asked me to sleep over, and his parents said it was OK, it was OK.

In the small apartment above his parents' butcher shop, our friendship went from playful and boyish to serious and grown-up. He locked the door to his room, and after that I didn't remember any words—just being quiet. We had to be very, very quiet. We were both mature for our age and responsible enough to be trusted with challenging roles in serious, adult theater productions. That's the only way this could happen. *This* was not being fooled around with by the bellhop or cuddling with my cousin but rather a full sexual expression of real feelings. With Walter, an intelligent, thoughtful, fellow actor, I learned that sex could be connected to love.

My friendship with Walter, which deepened over the course of the show and beyond, was of pure trust and affection; I loved him, and I knew he loved me. But I also knew that to others our love would be a disgrace.

The contradiction between those two realities didn't make sense, but it was my life, so I made it make sense by keeping my love for Walter a secret isolated in his bedroom and other private places. When I left to go home, the experience disappeared (or at least receded) so I could freely return to being Mother's pet, performing for friends who had come over to the house for mah-jongg. In this way I kept my life neatly compartmentalized. At school, I adopted the persona of the class clown to stay in the bullies' good graces. At the Play House, however, I was as serious as any grown-up professional theater actor. I tailored my behavior to each group, so I could give the people what they wanted. It was exhausting. It takes a lot of work to keep everything separate, but just like any other skill, the more you do it, the easier it becomes.

Me as an actor in the high school production of *Good News*.

CHAPTER THREE

Mother, all dressed up in a stylish suit and cloche—with faux grapes—that she had made the night before, was surrounded by a mountain of luggage and the Families Katz and Epstein. It was a brutal 10 degrees on that day in 1945 on the Union Terminal platform where she, Ronnie, and I (also all dressed up) waited to board a gigantic streamliner, but she was happy and excited. Like Rose from *Gypsy* who sang that she would "get my kids out," Grace was getting out of Cleveland.

Mother's expectation of a better, more glamorous life was finally coming true. My father had been hired to play with Spike Jones and His City Slickers; we were moving to Los Angeles. Hollywood, the land of her beloved movie stars!

This was Dad's really big break, Mother explained to The Sisters, who were not only freezing but also dying of envy. Mickey Katz had first come to the attention of Spike, the popular bandleader and major recording star, because of his musical expertise and unique gift of the "glug"—a percussive sound made by swallowing air. It was something impossible to teach; you either had it or you didn't. Spike was known for his satirical versions of famous pop and classical music using funny sounds such as horns, gunshots, and soon Dad's glug. One of his biggest hits, "Cocktails for Two," featured a chorus of hiccups and glugs. When Spike's orchestra toured, Dad was given clarinet solos and comedy bits to do, so that by the time he went out to California ahead of us to find an apartment, he was no longer just a Cleveland musician but one getting a national reputation.

As we boarded the train, I was shut down and sad. I didn't care about leaving school, friends, relatives, anything, or anyone in Cleveland—other than the Play House and Walter. I wondered if I would ever find another place where I seemed to belong as much. And as to the excitement, tenderness, and trust I shared with Walter, well, the thought of saying goodbye to that made me absolutely miserable. So I didn't really say goodbye to Walter; instead I told him I'd be back, even though I didn't know if I would.

I mourned privately as we pulled out of the station and Cleveland quickly receded into the distance. The novelty of the train trip—which included a dining car where anything you wanted was brought in silver service to tables covered in starched white tablecloths by elegant and smiling black gentlemen in full uniform—provided some distraction. Traveling more than 2,000 miles through Kansas and the Southwest, I watched America go by. Yet, no matter how deep the canyons or lovely the plains, I couldn't shake the feeling that a big and very important part of my nearly fourteen years was receding into the distance, too.

Los Angeles was a balmy 75 degrees, as if by movie magic. From the moment we stepped onto the platform at LA's fabled Union Station, where my teary, smiling father was waiting for us in a summer-weight suit, it was as if we had arrived in a foreign country. Together, the four of us click-clacked our way across the slippery terra-cotta-tiled floor, under a ceiling that seemed to reach the sky. We moved on past fountains, courtyards, and lush, enclosed garden patios. Things were growing everywhere, palms in the shape of giant fans, plants that looked like something out of the *Encyclopædia Britannica,* and flowers that were as red as Aunt Fritzi's lipstick.

In the twilight, Dad drove west on Wilshire Boulevard. Ronnie and I craned our heads out the windows to look at the palm trees that lined the streets en route to our new apartment. My father proudly announced "6148½ Orange Street!" as if it were the Taj Mahal. But by that time, it was totally dark. The Spanish Colonial architecture that had just an hour earlier appeared magical and inviting now seemed shadowy and strange. I never liked arriving in new destinations at night. (I still don't; the dark on top of unfamiliar rooms and furniture is doubly disorienting.) But after we had our Jell-O and milk, Ronnie and I went to our new room and fell asleep in our new twin beds.

I awoke at dawn to the most amazing, powerful, and sweet smell filling the entire room. Looking out the window, and through the filtered early-morning sunlight, I saw a real, live orange tree. The fruit dangled from a branch no more than a foot from my bed, so close that I couldn't believe what I saw. I put my hand right through the open window and pulled one off before loudly whispering, "Ronnie! Wake up. Look at this!" I stuck my amazing find right under his nose. "You can't do this in Cleveland!" I said as I tore the peel from the fruit and shared the prize with my baby brother.

We were all completely seduced by California: the sun, the flowers, the food. The *food!* The legendary Farmers Market, a bazaar of delicious and unusual things to eat at the corner of Third and Fairfax, was only six blocks north of us. The market was big enough for us to get lost in and brimming with produce. Mother picked, plucked, and prodded; since she was Grandpa Epstein's favorite daughter, fresh fruits and vegetables were nothing new. The real adventure was the stalls along the whole perimeter of the market, which served every kind of exotic cuisine.

Seated at outdoor picnic tables, we tasted so many new things. Mother, being the daring cook that she was, always encouraged Ronnie and me to try food that other kids wouldn't go near. We discovered cellophane noodles and sheer dumplings filled with juicy shrimp and pork; house-made hams and salamis piled atop buttered dark brown bread from the Danish stall; and Mexican tacos of pork butt that was both tender and crispy inside warm white flour tortillas, topped with a mixture of cilantro, onions, and lime. Nobody had ever heard of tacos in Cleveland, let alone tasted them.

The most electrifying aspect to our new life, however, was the fact that in LA the movies were *it*. They were the local pastime and industry. After seeing *Till the Clouds Roll By*, a big musical with June Allyson, Judy Garland, and Lena Horne, I became a huge fan of MGM's musicals and wanted to know all things Metro Goldwyn Mayer. I would always noodge my mom to take me to its Culver City lot. There, after telling her she had to park out of sight and stay in the car, I would stand by the big drive-in gate waiting with my autograph book for any stars exiting the lot. When we eventually moved into a house of our own, I covered the walls of my bedroom with photographs cut out from *Photoplay* of the biggest movie stars of the day—Gene Kelly, Fred Astaire, Mickey Rooney, Esther Williams, and Judy Garland.

Even school, with lunch eaten outdoors, had an air of glamour. When we arrived in LA, in the middle of the semester, it was more than a little intimidating, all that sizing-you-up stuff, and having my baby brother in tow did little to help my confidence. I was short and didn't play sports—and I now no longer had the Play House as a second home. Trying to figure out who I was in this new place, I remained quiet and careful until I better understood the lay of the land.

As I entered ninth grade at Alexander Hamilton High, confusion over my sexual identity only grew. I always liked girls a lot—and high school was no different. In many ways, I was more comfortable in their company than I was with boys. Girls were cute and fun—and they weren't competitive. Plus, they really liked me back. When I was little they liked me because I was good at jump rope. When I got older it was because I was a pretty good dancer. I had always danced with Mother ("You know your mother loves to dance") at home, to the radio, or whenever we went to see my father play. Whether I wanted to or not, I was her partner. I could do all the dances of the day, the rumba, the fox-trot, and the waltz, but the jitterbug, specifically swing dancing, was my favorite. Over the next two years, more and more of the girls of Hami High wanted to be around me because I could dance. It was what they had in mind besides dancing that I wasn't prepared for.

Things with girls always seemed to be started by them, even as far back as age seven when little Mary Ann from next door suggested I touch her somewhere I knew I shouldn't, and then put her hand in my pants (afterward, she told her mother, who called my mother, who gave me a boarding-school-level beating). Whether I was trying to prove something or simply be friendly, I always felt obligated to respond to advances made by girls I liked. That was definitely the case with Francine, the first girl I ever had sex with.

The feelings I had for Francine were that of compassion bordering on pity. I felt bad for her because her parents couldn't take care of her so she lived in a facility in Culver City run by Jewish services. She wasn't particularly pretty, but she had a big crush on me and never stopped calling my house.

As if it were an inevitability, Francine and I went out on a date. I picked her up in my father's new Hudson, drove along the coast—the grown-up thing to do—and parked in an abandoned lot by the beach, where we moved to the backseat. Without a word, she took all her clothes off; I didn't. When we began necking, perhaps the most powerful sensation I experienced was the smell of her acne medicine.

We had sex a couple of times back then, but it always felt dutiful. All of my experiences with girls lacked the passion, pleasure, and reciprocity I had had with Jerry and Walter. I was being a good sport and doing what was expected of me when her advances made the situation clear. Boys were supposed to want to have sex with girls. Everybody knew that. I had to prove that I was normal. To whom? I don't know. I guess myself.

All of my high school sexual experiences had a similar air of compliance even when the girl was a real knockout, such as Janet. She was a cheerleader all the jocks were crazy to date, but I was the one with whom she went out on a few dates. One day I stopped by her house to see if she wanted to go to Tom Crumplar's in Westwood Village for a malt, but she wasn't home. Still, her mother asked me if I wanted to come in. She looked more like her gorgeous older sister than like her mom. "Would you like something to drink?" she asked. "Lemonade, a Coke. Or a beer?"

A beer. Wow.

"Sure, I'll take a beer," I said coolly.

She smelled really good as she sat down next to me on the couch. We chatted for a couple of minutes while I sipped the beer. She moved her hand on my leg. Inwardly, I was alarmed. This was Janet's mom and I wasn't even an upperclassman! But the people-pleaser in me wasn't going to embarrass her by removing her hand. And the performer, the one who responded to almost any dare, took the situation a step further, moving in for a kiss.

I have always had an attraction to danger—furtive fumblings in the elevator, a secret rendezvous above the butcher shop—that translates easily into sexual provocation. Janet's mom clearly picked up on this vibe. Having a beer and sex with a beautiful and experienced older woman, who also happened to be my girlfriend's mother, was thrilling. What I did with Janet's mom, however, wasn't as intense as anything I did with Walter.

My self-doubt became acute. The notion that some people might be attracted to both boys and girls was totally outside the bounds of anything I had ever heard. The ambiguity I felt didn't seem like a choice. I definitely didn't want to face the idea that what really made me feel connected and truly sexually alive was sleeping with men, which was definitely not OK. And so I felt forced to hide in the uncertainty of it all. I knew that absolutely no one would understand.

I had found a comfortable place for myself in the scene at Hami High, which from the outside looked like the perfect brick high school in an MGM musical, even though it was in an iffy neighborhood. Iron-ically enough, my best friends were the jocks. These handsome, popu-lar, athletic lettermen turned me into their mascot. They kept an eye out for me against bullies (because of my small size and the conspicuous clothes Mother always made sure I wore, I was an easy target). The jocks liked having me around, because I knew how to entertain. The performing instinct—the one that brought me attention from Mr. Lowe at the Play House or walking down the aisle of my aunt's wedding—served me well in high school. I understood that people had expecta-tions of me, and not only did I comply, I amplified it.

I made the lettermen laugh with my impressions of teachers and other students just like my dad amusing his bandmates back at the Pal-ace. I was voted vice president of my class and became a member of the debate team. But I was no angel. When the occasion required it, I had no trouble being provocative. I pushed the limits, sometimes dangerously.

When Mrs. Mabel Montague, my drama teacher, who thought I had *something*, gave me carte blanche to direct a play of my own choice, I picked *The Lady of Larkspur Lotion*. This gritty one-act play centers on a woman who, having fallen on hard times, is living in a squalid boardinghouse, where she is reduced to prostitution as a way of avoid-ing eviction. The play, however well written and performed, was out-there and, as such, it stirred up a fair bit of controversy, shocking those who saw it—especially the school principal. My artistic efforts earned me a trip to his office, where he angrily asked, "Mr. Katz, what is this?"

My reply—"It's Tennessee Williams, one of our greatest playwrights"—got me sent home.

I was basically a show-off, and occasionally it got me into really big trouble. When everybody stopped to watch my stunning date Shirley Scharf and me do the jitterbug at a school dance that we had with Venice High, I felt like we were Judy Garland and Mickey Rooney. But as soon as the number was over, a tough-looking Mexican kid from the other school approached me on the dance floor to say, "I hear you called me a son of a bitch."

"No, I never said that."

"Are you saying my friend's a liar?"

"No. I'm not saying that. I just . . ."

"You want to come outside?"

"No. I don't want to come outside. I didn't say anything. Honest."

My exuberance on the dance floor with a beautiful blonde had enraged him.

I took Shirley's hand and slowly walked us to one of the exits, where we were blocked by two of his friends. We turned and walked, quickly now, to another exit, where we found two more guys closing in. There was no way out. I was sweating. I turned around for a second, but too late—the guy threw a punch and knocked me out. I awoke in Shirley's arms with a real shiner. Just like in the movies.

Friday-night services at the Westside Jewish Congregation were filled with professional upper-middle-class worshippers, mostly from the cold, windy Eastern cities, who six months earlier had turned the airy Protestant church into a conservative synagogue. The Brentwood congregation, which my family had joined, was nothing like the dark and serious Orthodox shul, Chabad Yerushalaim, in Cleveland where I was bar mitzvahed just days before our moving to LA.

The white stucco Spanish Colonial Revival building, surrounded by beds of bright-orange California poppies, was beautiful, but the real draw of the synagogue was Paul Gold, the charismatic twenty-five-year-old cantor, who captivated everyone. Even Mother, who was never particularly interested in anything Jewish, paid close attention as he cast a spell over the sanctuary while welcoming the Sabbath with a prayer that struck a peculiar combination of joy and melancholy.

After the service, everyone would crowd into the community room in the basement for kosher wine, challah, and rugelach. Reciting the blessings over the wine and bread, adoring members gathered around their cantor, who was tall, dark, handsome—and single. There wasn't a woman in the room who hadn't tried to set him up. Everyone agreed:

A man who took his job seriously but was also accessible, funny, had killer good looks, was a catch, and then some.

Like everyone else at Westside, I was enthralled with Paul. So when after chatting with my folks for some time, he turned to me and said, "Your mother tells me *you* sing, too," I felt my cheeks burn with a heady mixture of connection and disbelief. To have this good-looking, sought-after man single out me, some dopey sixteen-year-old, for attention was almost too much to take. My parents looked over at us, beaming over the fact that such a man was showing interest in their talented son!

"If I can ever help you with your singing," he said, "I'm always here."

It would have been rude not to take him up on his generous offer. A few days later I came by the WJC after school. He was just leaving but asked me if I'd like to go across the street to have a coffee. "Or is that too grown-up?" he said.

My cheeks started burning again. But over coffee, we talked and laughed with each other easily. He knew a lot about vocal technique and had majored in theater at college.

I stopped by the center for coffee a few times until once, after I walked him to his car, he said, "Get in. I'll give you a lift." When we got into the car, we sat there for what seemed like an eternity. I could feel him staring at me but for some reason was afraid to turn my head and meet his gaze. The electricity that had been turned on since the moment I caught his attention during kiddish in the basement of the synagogue was now kicking in. Before I grew uncomfortable, he smiled and put an easy arm around my shoulder. In that moment, when a romantic encounter with him went from a fantasy to a possibility, I became an equal player. Our attraction was mutual. I really wanted this, despite how taboo it was because of his position, age, and gender. And now I knew that he wanted it, too. With my excitement clear, Paul moved the seat that went across the entire front of the car back so that we had more room.

We started spending a lot of time together (slowly my "singing" improved). Despite the danger, we met several times a week, at his place or office, in the car, at the movies, anywhere anonymous or absolutely private. Of course, he always took top priority in my plans. I wanted to be with Paul all the time.

Naturally I kept all the details of our friendship secret; we had to be very careful. Whether a rite of passage in a young person's growth toward independence or a necessity given the wrath that would be my punishment, I had learned earlier in my life to lie really well to my parents and others about where I was going and whom I was seeing. And so no one ever challenged me or suspected a thing.

I felt completely safe with Paul, so much so that even when he suggested that we go horseback riding at Will Rogers Park in the Santa Monica Mountains I wasn't terribly concerned. My only experience with horses was being photographed seated on a pony, wearing a red-and-white kerchief round my neck, at the age of five. I told Paul that I didn't ride, but he was very reassuring, explaining that these horses were gentle and besides, *he* was very experienced. "Don't worry," he said. And I didn't worry; I never worried with Paul. While I felt as much connection to Paul as I had with Walter, there was no comparison. Although Walter was older than I, he was still my contemporary. Paul, however, was a figure of authority and experience.

The 186 acres of land overlooking the Pacific Ocean had once been home to the much-loved humorist, vaudeville cowboy, newspaper columnist, and legendary actor but was left to the state by his widow. Paul rented horses for us from the stables, mounting his expertly. With a boost from one of the cowboys at the park, I soon sat tall on a big beautiful horse and pretended all was well, as I often did. I wasn't exactly relaxed, but I was with Paul, and his confidence was not only reassuring, it boosted my own. After about a half hour, with Paul leading at only a slow trot, we left the trail and went into the more densely wooded area.

Being among the trees with no one else around was like being in a movie. I was starting to enjoy the ride. When we found ourselves in a clearing, we climbed down, and Paul tied the horses to a tree. We got right to setting up the blanket. Even as deep into the woods as we were, there was still the slight chance that we could be discovered. But the risk only heightened the moment. He had hidden a split of champagne in his jacket pocket. While he was tying the horses to a tree, I put my arms around him. Paul turned around and as he began to unbutton my shirt, I opened his belt. Naked atop the blanket, I thought, *So* this *was grown-up passion*, what caring and being cared for felt like.

Our relationship had to be a secret, but I never doubted that it was real. Although I was dating girls at school, Paul became my obsession. With him I was at my most. Not to say I didn't experience pleasure with girls, but there were just so many more levels to the pleasure I had with Paul. In turn, he was attentive, passionate, and seemingly sincere. So when Linda, a friend from the temple, whispered in confidence to me during Friday-night services that she had a "crush" on Paul, I genuinely felt bad for her. Not that she wasn't attractive, because she was. In fact, Linda had everything: looks, intelligence, and a wealthy family (her parents were big donors to the synagogue).

Although my dad had become more and more successful as a musician and comedian, you would never consider us well-to-do. During Dad's lean periods, we moved a lot; all of us once crammed into a one-room apartment over a garage for a few weeks. But Dad finally saved enough for a down payment on a small, pale-green ranch house in the city's Palms neighborhood. I loved that house on Malcolm Avenue where we had not only had a victory garden but also a fox terrier we named Lulu.

Still, it was nothing compared with Linda's family and their Beverly Hills mansion. She would pick me up after school sometimes in her white Oldsmobile convertible—all the jocks whistling and shouting catcalls. Whenever the gorgeous nineteen-year-old arrived at the school with the top down, my stock at Hami went way up.

It never occurred to me, though, that Paul would be the least bit interested. She'd go on and on, mooning over him, and planning an attack to win his affections.

And then they started to date.

When I realized that it was really happening, I was stunned and promptly came down with the flu. I didn't answer the dozens of calls from either of them. Linda thought it was because I was sick, but Paul knew. After a few weeks, I finally took his call; he assured me that nothing had changed. He still loved me—and he wanted to see me despite his new girlfriend. "Yes, I'm seeing her, but you are the most important person in my life," he said. I understood what he was saying, because being with women was part of my life, too. It was the way of the world. You had to go out with girls to function in society. "Linda is also fond of you," he added.

Unfortunately, I wasn't able to stay away from him, and so our affair became ever more complicated and torturous. Knowing he was with Linda and lying to her, all the while still needing him, was hard. So this was grown-up love.

Their romance, which was the talk of West LA, quickly became serious.

"Paul and Linda. Aren't they wonderful together!"

"She has money and beauty, and he's so intelligent and inspiring."

"And to think that they fell in love right before our eyes."

While everyone congratulated themselves on the wonderful news, I was stunned—betrayed and confused. How was this possible? And yet, just as when I had left Walter behind in Cleveland, there was no one to turn to, no one to tell. The times, my age, Paul's profession, and his own need to remain closeted all meant that I had to suffer in silence. To whom could I even tell such a thing? Isolation was a terrible by-product of keeping secrets. When they announced their wedding, slated to be a big social event of the season, I thought, *If they only knew.*

Not long after they were married, Linda called to ask if I would join them for dinner. At Musso & Frank in Hollywood, the three of us shared one of the booths in the restaurant's dark wood interior. When we finished the meal, it was still early. Paul, excited about a new Horowitz recording, suggested that we all go back to their apartment to listen to it. At their place, he put on the record before disappearing into the kitchen. He reemerged with champagne to celebrate the three of us being together again. He toasted to how much we all loved one another, and we drank to being friends forever.

Paul was a little overly solicitous and exuberant, but I assumed it was discomfort over my being in the presence of his new wife. He lowered the lights. "A little mood lighting for Mr. Horowitz," he said, sliding in between Linda and me on the couch and putting an arm around each of us.

It took about three sips for the champagne to go to my head. The notes of the Chopin etude tripped along warm air. This wasn't so bad. Then, he turned his face toward mine and kissed me. Linda might have been as surprised as I was; I had no idea, because I stared straight ahead and didn't dare look anywhere near her direction for a reaction. Then it was my turn to be surprised when Paul turned to kiss her. Paul, our cantor, her husband, my lover, started to undress Linda while I sat there and watched. The whole thing was so mixed up that it went way past shock. Paul, taking my hand and putting it on Linda's breast, set into motion a scenario that I willingly went along with. The last thing I wanted to be around Paul was an unsophisticated kid. When it was all over, I realized I'd better get home. I had school the next day and hadn't studied for a math test. Someone drove me home. I don't remember who.

After that night I no longer saw or heard from Paul or Linda. I stopped going to services (whenever my parents asked if I was coming I found myself busy). The shame of what we had done together was too great for me to face, and I assumed that the same was true for them. About four months after our night together, though, Linda showed up at school. She still had the white convertible, but when she came this time the top was up. "I can't any . . . more," she told me, her eyes red from crying. "He's started bringing guys home, strangers and . . . I just can't." While we were sitting in the car, Linda explained to me how she had told her parents everything; they wanted to get her an annulment and drive Paul out of town. I realized her position was not unlike mine. Having someone you love so much quickly become someone else is terrifying.

But then, behind the wheel of her Oldsmobile, Linda told me something that took my breath away. Her lawyer, who was acting quickly, spoke about naming me as a co-respondent. Hearing this was perhaps the most frightening moment of my life. My heart didn't just sink; it plummeted. It was a problem I was not only far too young to handle, it was also something without precedent, something I couldn't have imagined in my worst nightmares. One thing I knew for certain: My life was over. But the worst part was that I was going to take my family down with me. A story so sordid and sensational would surely be picked up by the press, and then the whole town would know that Mickey Katz, a rising and beloved star in the music scene, had raised a lowlife deviant. Everything Dad had worked so hard for, down the drain because of me. The Sisters had been right after all: I was bad.

Telling my parents was the last thing I wanted to do, but having them learn it in the press would have been even worse. After Linda dropped me off, I walked into the house and found Mom doing dishes and Dad practicing. I asked them to come into the living room—I needed to talk to them. By this time I was crying. I was in terrible trouble. I told them the truth about Paul and me, the night with Linda, and now the annulment.

The look that swept across my parents' faces solidified my guilt into a giant mass pressing down upon my chest, making it hard for me to breathe. The three of us stood there for what seemed forever, stunned by the scope of all of it—this unthinkable, unimaginable nightmare that nevertheless we all were beginning to process as truth. Finally, my dad turned to look at my mom, then at me. But Mother's eyes never strayed; they bore into me with cold contempt as I wept. I reached out for her, sobbing, "I'm sorry," but she drew back.

"Don't ever touch me again," she said. "You disgust me."

She had hurt me many ways and many times before, but nothing she had ever done or said had even come close to this.

Once my father and I were alone, he put his arm around me without hesitation.

"Let's go for a ride, sonny," he said.

After driving around in silence for what seemed like a lifetime, Dad and I both staring straight ahead, he said, "She doesn't mean it. She's your mother, she loves you, I know she loves you." But I knew in that moment life for my mother and I had been forever altered.

The affair fortunately never became public, and I didn't have to testify. Linda got her annulment and moved on with her life, and Paul disappeared off the face of the Earth. Although I was still living in the same house, going to the same school, wearing the same clothes, my life was changed. My mother had shown me her last act of coldness, and I vowed never to need her again. I had to let her go.

Having been betrayed by Paul *and* my mother, two adults I loved very much, I wondered who I could trust. The answer was clear: only me. My mother turned away from me—literally running away—when I needed her most. Now I needed to take care of myself.

I didn't want the audience to think I got the job just 'cause
I was the boss's kid.

CHAPTER FOUR

Dressed in a ten-gallon hat, woolly chaps, and a borscht-colored cow-boy shirt with BAR MITZVAH RANCH emblazoned across it, my father did his best imitation of an Arkansas hog caller by way of Chelm. Audience members clapped to the frenetic klezmer tune and laughed to the point of tears as Dad performed his hit "Yiddish Square Dance."

> *Yiddle mitten fiddle*
> *Yankel mitten bass*
> *Cum shpilt a little*
> *Oifen mitten gahs*

Seated in the center of the third row, I was struck by the juxtaposition of the ecstatic Jewish audience and the refined, decidedly not-at-all-Jewish theater in which my father put it on. The Wilshire Ebell, in the tony neighborhood of Hancock Park, was originally a women's club that dated from the nineteenth century, ancient history by LA standards. The mahogany-paneled theater, which the society ladies rented out for cultural events, was an odd goyish atmosphere for such a totally haimish celebration. This theater—where a young Judy Garland was discovered singing with her sisters—now hosted my dad's English-Yiddish stage revue, *Borscht Capades*.

The show—which played every weekend night (the only nights the theater was rentable) to sold-out audiences—was the brainchild of Father's canny manager and childhood friend, Hal Zeiger, who was looking to capitalize on the success of Dad's first hit song. "Haim Afen Range," my father's Yiddish parody of "Home on the Range," was the most unlikely chart-topper in *Billboard* history.

Even as a teenager, Dad always liked to write parodies, such as "Little Red Rosenberg," for fun. But it wasn't until a happy accident occurred during a recording session for Spike Jones that he considered them anything more than a way of entertaining his friends and family. During a break in the session, my father sang one of his parodies for a Jewish trumpet player, who laughed until he could barely breathe. Dad didn't know that the mike was open, and that the RCA executives in the control room were also listening. Even though they were Gentile and didn't understand a word of Yiddish, they found the sounds and idea of Yiddishizing a classic American song so hysterical that they suggested he make a Yiddish comedy single.

Dad threw himself into the project. To record "Haim Afen Range," he gathered the very best from the world of Jewish musicians, including his friend and composer Al Sack. Al, a fellow Clevelander and the musical director for Dinah Shore's radio show, wrote the song's musical arrangement. The elite musicians, who typically played the scores for the biggest movie studios of the day, performed "Haim Afen Range" as if their souls had been yearning for it. They were thrilled to play the music of their forefathers instead of the theme to *Ben-Hur*. When Dad heard the final product, he realized some kind of magic had been created and quickly wrote "Yiddish Square Dance" for the flip side of the record.

His instincts turned out to be right on the money. In the fall of 1947, RCA released 10,000 copies in New York City, and the 78 rpm recording sold out in three days—with orders for 25,000 more! The record eventually hit upward of 200,000 copies. Mickey Katz had a smash! On the heels of its meteoric sales, Colony Records played my dad's first solo record from loudspeakers that blared onto Broadway.

Oy geb mir a haim
(oh, give me a home)

Mit a viabele shain
(with a pretty wife)

Vu de sheps und die tziggelach lafen
(where the sheep and lambs run)

Oy geb mir a hois
(oh, give me a house)

Mit gesundte cowboys
(with healthy cowboys)

Und a por hundred cattle tzu far kafen
(and a couple of hundred cattle to sell)

Hundreds of people of every ethnicity walking down Broadway stopped to listen to the virtuosic freilach and Dad's outrageous delivery. Jew, Irish, Italian, black—it sounded funny to everyone even if they, like the original RCA execs who commissioned the album, didn't totally understand it.

Dad was thrilled, and so was Mom, who found validation in all the attention and opportunity that song brought. This one hit made it clear that Mickey was going places, which is what she always thought about him, even when he was just a sixteen-year-old horn-blower in Cleveland. Dad's newfound success couldn't have come at a better time for my mother. True to my word, I kept my distance from her after the cantor affair. It had been months after the Paul and Linda drama before I could even be in the same room with her. In the space left by my emotional absence came this big new presence: fame. She was getting what she needed, and she did need it.

On the heels of "Haim Afen Range," RCA Victor offered my father a recording contract. "Tico, Tico"—the song recorded and made famous by Carmen Miranda after she performed it in the film *Copacabana*—became "Tickle, Tickle." The Spike Jones hit "Chloe" was Yiddishized into "Chloya."

"Barber of Schlemiel," "That Pickle in the Window," and "She'll Be Coming 'Round the Katzkills" were more than just entertaining. In light of the larger geopolitical events raging around him—World War II and the Holocaust—Dad's zany little songs were actually an act of bravery. There was a tremendous amount of fear in being Jewish, even in the US, which was far from immune to anti-Semitism. Many American Jews, particularly those who had found success, wanted to assimilate, not highlight their background. This was a time when there were still Gentile-only country clubs, law firms, and hospitals. We were here but not entirely welcome.

Yiddish for some Jews was death. My father breathed life back into it, and for that he was considered by many to be a hero. But my father didn't record his parodies just because he thought it would be good for the Jews. Though he loved the idea of giving people a sense of their heritage, because he was so proud of it himself, his sense of humor drove his music. Yet by parodying the hit songs of the day—such as "Shrimp Boats" (it became "Herring Boats") and "Kiss of Fire" ("Kiss of Meyer")—which everyone, both Jew and Gentile, knew, he was inviting the larger American society into the beauty and hilarity of Jewish culture. He was inserting Jews into pop culture, so that we belonged, too.

From the moment "Haim Afen Range" hit, his life turned around. Mickey Katz became a bona fide recording star. So in 1948, when he and Hal worked on the idea for *Borscht Capades*, Dad was of course the draw, the headliner. Hal, who became one of the first big promoters of rock in the fifties, later represented and promoted everyone from

Frank Zappa to Lenny Bruce to Ray Charles. In this period, he was devoted to my dad even though they were complete opposites. Hal, who towered over my small, slight father, was a tough guy, while there was no bigger softy than my father. Hal was the muscle, the businessman, and liked taking care of Dad.

Up until this point, Dad never had to carry a show. Other than the occasional bit he did while part of the Palace orchestra in Cleveland, such as the one where he played Jean Harlow's cuckolded lover, Dad was at heart a musician—not an actor, personality, or emcee. But this was the time of *The Ed Sullivan Show*, when people expected a host to guide them through an evening's entertainment. That meant he had to entertain not only by playing his hits but also by introducing the acts. He had to become a master of ceremonies.

Funny and sweet, he proved to be a great emcee—even if he didn't love the part. He would have preferred simply to play with his band, because that was his passion. Yet his desire and his temperament, self-deprecating without acting the fool, made him a natural.

Borscht Capades became the talk of LA, from Beverly Hills to Boyle Heights—it was *that* good. The revue offered something that couldn't be found anywhere else. For all those people who had no place to hear klezmer music, Yiddish humor, and freilachs, the Wilshire Ebell was it.

The show had something for everyone: Women swooned over a handsome tenor singing "*Ich hob dir tzu fil leibt*" ("I love you much too much"); men laughed at the ventriloquist Rickie Layne and his Yiddish-speaking dummy, Velvel; and everyone stood solemnly when Dad and his six-piece band ended the show with Israel's national anthem, "Hatikvah." Tickets became a hot commodity with scalpers selling them for top dollar. Meanwhile, my father, whose home number was listed in the phone book, took reservations from the public from our living room.

"Hello, I'd like to speak to Mickey about tickets," a woman said when I answered the phone. Everyone called him Mickey, as if they knew him. I passed the receiver to my dad.

"Mrs. Goldberg, I have four seats in the fifth row," he said.

"This seat is going to be fine," he continued.

I didn't need to hear Mrs. Goldberg's side of the conversation to know what she was saying; everyone wanted to be in the first four rows. And they all had an excuse—a bad foot, bad hearing, a very important person from "the community." But who could fit all these people into the first four rows?

Our family always sat in the first four rows. Mother, all dressed up and gorgeous, was there every night in a different outfit, of course. She wouldn't miss an opportunity to take bows after the show as admirers came up to congratulate the lovely Mrs. Mickey Katz. And it wasn't just Mother; my aunts, uncles, and grandparents, all having followed our family out to LA, had to be at the show as well.

The Epsteins made the exodus to Hollywood at about the same time as my father's success with *Borscht Capades*. They had to make sure that Mother didn't have anything that they didn't have, too. Hearing about Grace's wonderful life was just too much for them to take—when they received the photos Mother had sent of herself in a bathing suit, posed like a screen siren in our backyard in February, they immediately sold everything in Cleveland and came out to California. The Sisters—who were all married by that time, even Beverly the baby—arrived on the West Coast within weeks of one another.

With husbands and kids in tow, they invaded the Westside, where we lived. There was Fritzi and her husband, Eddie Volk, and their two kids, Jackie and Robin (who later changed his name to Bobby). Helen and Irv, Burton's parents, started up a hamburger joint near the Farmers Market.

Grandpa Morris wasn't feeling well when he made the move, and not long afterward he was diagnosed with cancer from which he soon died. Fanny didn't waste any time grieving. A year later, she married Harry Brody, whom she schlepped along wherever she wanted, and took his name.

Dad's family, who came out after the Epsteins, also lived on the

Westside. (Between the Katzes and Epsteins, about forty citizens left Cleveland for good.) Abe, now Al, continued to work as a pharmacist, and Aunt Jeannie married Morris Schneider, whose religion and profession were both a little cloudy. Although it was a constant topic of family conversation, we never knew what Uncle Morris did for a living or if he was really Jewish. Esther and her husband Eddie opened Katz's Finer Foods, on Pico.

With the Westside colonized by my entire extended family, life in California shared a lot of similarities to what I knew back East. There was, however, one major exception: I no longer had a theater to act in.

Before we left Cleveland, K. Lowe recommended that my mom bring me to the Pasadena Playhouse, a historically important theater that mounted productions of Shakespeare as well as the Southern California premieres of works by Eugene O'Neill, F. Scott Fitzgerald, Noël Coward, and Tennessee Williams.

Located in a low 1920s Spanish Colonial Revival building around a gracious arcaded courtyard, the "talent factory," as it was known in LA, was certainly professional. I auditioned and landed a part in *Dear Octopus*, an English drawing-room comedy by the playwright and novelist Dodie Smith about three generations of a family, hoping that I might re-create my experience back in Cleveland. But the Play House was a once-in-a-lifetime opportunity that turned out to be impossible to replicate. With K., Miss Paxton, and the rest, I was not only inspired creatively but also nurtured emotionally. At the Pasadena Playhouse I was just in a play. After *Dear Octopus* finished its run, I didn't return.

I auditioned for some radio jobs. Radio was big, big, big back then. The one job I got was on *Red Ryder*, a radio show based on a popular Western comic strip. I was the understudy for Little Beaver, whose big line was "You betchum, Red Ryder." Otherwise, acting in school plays and working with Mrs. Montague composed the sum total of my acting experience in LA.

Sitting in the audience of the Wilshire Ebell and watching all the people around me cheer and laugh during *Borscht Capades* made me want to be onstage again. It would be great to join my dad's show, but I had never sung or danced onstage before, and I didn't know if I could do it.

I turned to my godmother, Aunt Jeannie, for help in finding a suitable number that might work for the revue. Whatever I did had to appeal to the Yiddishkeit-loving audience of *Borscht Capades* but also capitalize on my seventeen-year-old energy. Jeannie had just the thing. In her living room, she took out "Rumania, Rumania," a very popular song sung by Aaron Lebedoff, the Yiddish theater's answer to Danny Kaye, and placed the needle on the record:

Ay! Rumania, Rumania, Rumania . . .
Geven amol a land a zise, a sheyne.
Ay! Rumania, Rumania, Rumania . . .
Geven amol a land a zisseh, a fineh.

The fast-patter song exploded with a million Yiddish words. With dizzying speed, Lebedoff sang of a Romania from before the war, "a land, sweet and lovely" where "what your heart desires you can get; a mamalige, a pastrami, a karnatzl, and a glass of wine, aha!"

I had never spoken a word of Yiddish, so Aunt Jeannie translated the lyrics, which I wrote down in longhand. I also wrote down the phonetic sounds of the Yiddish words, which my aunt helped me decipher, and memorized them. It was very difficult and very fast. The song was a real Yiddish tongue twister, but I sensed it would make a great, great piece of material.

In quick succession, Dad figured out an orchestration for the number, I rehearsed it with the band, and that very same night, I was on. My one request was that he not say I was his son when he introduced me; I didn't want the audience to think I got the job because I was the boss's kid. So instead, my father announced, "And now, ladies and gentlemen, please welcome, Joel Kaye!"

I came out, and the audience smiled at me as they would for any other nice Jewish boy. What happened next was a blur. I improvised all my dance moves while trying to remember the torrent of foreign words. I pulled from Jerry Lewis, Danny Kaye, and Mickey Rooney. I crossed my eyes and puffed out my cheeks. No body part was left unused. I jumped; I growled. You couldn't exactly call it singing, but whatever it was, the audience loved it.

Clapping and singing along with the lyrics, they knew the song well. Its nostalgia for the vanished pleasures of the Old Country resonated with them. To have these Yiddish words usher from the mouth of a young person was the ultimate symbol of hope. Perhaps all that they once were was not lost. It was a showstopper.

When I was done, my heart pounding in my chest and sweat dripping down my forehead, the reaction from the crowd sounded like a helicopter's landing. They shouted and shrieked, "More! More!" What I got from the audience was a rush, like a drug. This was not *On Borrowed Time*.

With my one song over, my father took the stage and came over to me. Borrowing from the famous curtain speech coined by George M. Cohan—the legendary Broadway performer and founder of American musical comedy—Dad said, "Joel's mother thanks you. His brother thanks you. His Aunt Jean thanks you. And I'm his father. And I thank you, too." The audience went crazy.

From that moment on I was a bona fide member of *Borscht Capades*. Dad always introduced me the same way, respecting my initial wish to be identified as his son only after I finished my act. He did make one small modification. "Now, ladies and gentleman," he would say, "please welcome the Juvenile Star of *Borscht Capades*!" (To this day, my brother still kids me about it whenever he calls, asking, "Is the Juvenile Star of *Borscht Capades* home?)

I was an instant hit, but I needed another number. Dad, the writer, came to the rescue with "Yossel Yossel," a parody based on the Andrews Sisters' hit "Joseph! Joseph!"

When I was eight days old, they named me Yossel
Oh, what a simcha; such a celebration!
All my mishpuchah drank a toast l'chaim
while I was suffering a minor operation.
And later on, I went to kindergarten.
I said, "Teacher, Yossel is my name."
She said, "The name of Yossel, it sounds like a schlomossel."
From Yossel, my name became Joel Kaye.

"Yossel Yossel," "Rumania," and one more song Dad wrote for me about how much I loved the Jewish holidays became my act, fifteen sock-'em minutes of pure kvelling from the audience. I was everyone's darling—including Mother's.

"He's never sung or danced before. Can you imagine?" she'd say. "Oh, no, he doesn't speak a word of Yiddish. I don't know where he gets it from."

This was from the woman who had been so disgusted by and angry with me after she found out about my affair with the cantor that she wanted to send me to military school (an ironic choice, considering my crime). Now that I was getting a little bit of my own fame, all seemed to be forgiven. At least on her part. She could praise me to others as much as she wanted. No matter how much she tried to show affection toward me directly, I always kept a stiff arm. Mother was able to move on because, according to her, what had happened between Paul and me was relegated to the past. Right after the incident, instead of military school, she and my father had decided to send me to therapy.

It wasn't my first time in treatment. I had gone to see a psychologist at thirteen, not long after moving to LA, because I was having trouble with a bully and didn't want to go to school. Gertrude, the therapist, was civilized, intelligent, and compassionate, and I enjoyed talking to her in the little room in the garden in back of her house. I was able to discuss my feelings in a calm way I couldn't at home.

Freud believed that all human beings started out bisexual, eventually turning homosexual or heterosexual depending on their early family dynamic. Beginning in the 1940s, however, psychoanalytic theory for the most part considered homosexuality a pathology. Horrific treatments, including electroshock therapy, chemical castration, hormone injections, and even lobotomies, were widely used in an attempt to cure homosexuals of their mental illness.

I was incredibly lucky with Gertrude (as well as with the other few psychologists I would have in my lifelong relationship with therapy). When I talked frankly about the same-sex desires I was wrestling with, she didn't panic. I wasn't a bad person for the thoughts I had or even the things I had done. On the contrary, she told me I was smart, capable, sensible, and funny. My struggles were never black and white. Still, Gertrude framed my interest in men as developmental, something I would eventually get over with work and understanding. That's what I wanted, too.

I never discussed the sessions with my mom and dad. The girls I took out on dates after Paul had been run out of town were proof enough for my parents that I was "cured." My homosexual experiences could be chalked up to adolescent experimentation—at least as far as Mother was concerned, so why would I let her know otherwise. In fact, I didn't let her know anything.

Something fundamental had been broken between my mother and me. I saw her clearly for who she was, a painful experience but one out of which some good did come. From my earliest memories, my mother had led me to believe that my father was weak so that she could have me all to herself. ("Look at you. You're just like me; you're your mother's son.") After she shunned me, any distance that might have existed between my father and me closed. Although I always loved him,

I realized he was in fact a man of substance, someone I could rely upon no matter what.

So when my father decided to go on the road with *Borscht Capades*, there was no question that I wanted to go with him. The tour went to every city that had a decent-sized Jewish community. As we traveled to Chicago, Minneapolis, Cleveland, Boston, Phoenix, Toronto, Montreal, and elsewhere, I learned on the road that there were Jewish communities in places where I had never imagined they existed—I became fascinated with the American Indian Baskets, beaded vests, and silver buckles I found in trading posts . . . often owned by Jews.

I loved traveling, experiencing the best a city or town had to offer in museums, restaurants, and shops—not to mention the hotels, where they changed the linens every day. But the road was also lonely. While on tour with *Borscht Capades*, I missed my graduation, prom, and being with friends my own age.

Not only was everyone who came out to see *Borscht Capades* old—at least in my book (at that point, thirty-five seemed ancient). But everyone in the show was, too. I spent a lot of time with Rickie Layne, who at twenty-five was closest to my age, but I wasn't looking for someone to pal around with. I wanted to get laid, and even trickier, I wanted it to be with other young guys. Traveling with my father didn't make the chance of that happening at all possible.

But when *Borscht Capades* rolled into Miami Beach in January of 1950, sexuality hung in the balmy ocean air. The Art Deco District, or South Beach, as it came to be known throughout the world, was *the* happening place at that moment. Particularly if you were Jewish. On the stretch of beach just over the causeway from Miami, the ghetto of elderly Jews sitting in folding chairs playing mah-jongg or the balalaika had given way to a boom of enormous hotels springing up along Collins Avenue as fast as weeds. These lavish resorts, fueled by a postwar country flush with cash, gave their clientele the latest in modern comforts. The Bombay Hotel was the first in Miami Beach to offer its guests a parking garage. Later, the Fontainebleau (designed by the Russian Jewish architect Morris Lapidus, who did many of the hotels on what became known as Millionaire's Row) boasted the Staircase to Nowhere, a two-story staircase that led only to a coat check so that women, who had come up the elevators to deposit their coats, could make a grand descent into the lobby.

I loved it on the beach: the smell of Coppertone; couples decked out to stroll under the palm trees that lined the stretch of white sand; uniformed boys dashing in between with umbrellas with cocktails, soft drinks, and sandwiches for hotel guests. Men wearing guayaberas and smoking Cuban cigars played high-stakes poker games from private cabanas. Meanwhile, their wives, in full makeup, big hair, and even bigger diamonds, took cha-cha lessons by the hotel pool.

Over-the-top was part and parcel of Miami Beach, and *Borscht Capades* took it by storm. The show received unanimously rave reviews from all of Miami's newspapers. The Roosevelt Theatre—a thousand-seat movie house for which Hal Zeiger spent $4,000 to build a stage—was sold out every night. As my father described it in his memoir, *Papa Play for Me*, "The lines at the box office every day looked like a sale at Macy's."

Mom and Ronnie, still in high school, joined us in Miami, where Dad had arranged for us to stay at the Delano in South Beach. The three-year-old hotel had private beach cabanas equipped with telephones and hot showers; a sultry saltwater pool, where night swimming parties were not uncommon; and seventeen stories that made it the tallest tower in Miami. Thanks to Dad's friend and hotel manager Chuckie Goldberg, the Katz family was on top of the Delano for $35 a day.

Despite the family reunion, I was still able to find some fun of my own making. On most nights the show was at 8:30 P.M., which meant that I could still make it to the mambo contests after it ended. Most of the hotels held these events, where you could take lessons, compete, or simply soak in the sexy, dark atmosphere while getting drunk.

There were also plenty of gay bars that flourished in Miami's permissive environment. But I never went to them. I was Mickey Katz's son, now in his successful show. I couldn't even consider going to any place as dangerous as a gay bar. First of all, I was terrified of being arrested, which was happening to people all the time. It was 1950, and homosexuality was considered a criminal act. But if the media found me out, it would be almost as bad. I would bring shame upon my family, ruin my father's run, and end any future for myself. If I hadn't known it already, the experience of revealing my affair with the cantor to my parents proved that nobody, not even those most likely to love me regardless of my actions, could accept that part of me.

I found my pleasure in a much more intimate place. Although I felt men's eyes cruising me everywhere—an act that for many gay men leads quickly and directly to sex—I needed a partner who also risked losing everything if he told. That turned out to be the hotel's masseur. He worked in the hotel's solarium on the top floor. There the spa, encased in glass, led to terraces outside, where men on chaise lounges that had been covered in great white sheets because of the heat liked to sunbathe naked and drink Cuba libres. So when this muscled, bodybuilder-type masseur in his white uniform gave me a look, I knew it was safe. If he ever said a word about us to anyone, he would never work in Miami again.

With my masseur and packed audiences every night, I already felt like the toast of the town. But then one day, news arrived at our hotel suite that made everything else seem bland: Eddie Cantor was coming to *Borscht Capades* that night, specifically to see *me*. Mr. Cantor had a big reputation for discovering new talent. If he named you one of his "stars of tomorrow," it could really mean something.

Like my Dad, Mr. Cantor had combined his talent with ambition to raise himself out of hardscrabble beginnings. Although he became one of the most successful comedians in vaudeville history, Mr. Cantor started out from the tenements of Manhattan's Lower East Side, where he was orphaned at the age of one. But just as Dad did, he performed in and usually won amateur contests for his impressions. His pay grew along with his talent. His salary as a featured player in the *Ziegfeld Follies* alongside one of his best friends, Will Rogers, prompted the impresario Florenz Ziegfeld to call Mr. Cantor the highest-paid comedian "in the history of the world."

By the time I had come to his attention, through the owners of Grossinger's, the legendary Jewish resort in the Catskills, where I had performed a number of times, Mr. Cantor had already transitioned from the dying world of vaudeville. Radio was the beginning of the demise of vaudeville, which was the most popular entertainment in America during the turn of the century. Like many big vaudevillians such as Burns and Allen, Bob Hope, and Will Rogers, Mr. Cantor had gone where the work was—first to radio, then the movies, and now, the new medium of television. He was in Florida as part of a nationwide hunt for fresh talent to appear on his new TV show.

Keenly aware that he was in the audience at the Roosevelt that night, I gave *Rumania, Rumania* my all. If I got on TV, I was told, people would know my name, and I would become a commodity. That would help pave the way for more jobs as an actor—ideally in the theater. That muggy Miami night, I was auditioning for the most important job of my life.

After the show, Mr. Cantor came backstage to say he'd like to introduce me on his upcoming television show, *The Colgate Comedy Hour*.

My family was thrilled. Dad said this was my "big chance," even though Hal was opposed to it. *The Colgate Comedy Hour* meant I had to leave *Borscht Capades* to work on new material in LA for the TV show. Losing me could be bad for business, but Dad insisted he was "for it all the way." He always wanted the best for me. I knew my mother was thrilled even though she didn't say anything at all on the topic. Staying quiet wasn't like Mom. But I understood that she didn't want to be effusive about the opportunity, since it was a loss for Dad's show. However, if she hadn't liked the idea, Mother definitely would have spoken up. Grace was nothing if not a realist. *Borscht Capades* was limited in its appeal because it was for a Jewish audience. TV's audience was unlimited.

I finished out the last two weeks of our run at the Roosevelt, left for California, and then, on April 1, 1951, found myself back East to perform live on national TV. *The Colgate Comedy Hour*, which we did in Philadelphia, was a storm of technology and terror—at least for me. Heaps of wire coiled around like snakes, and enormous cameras pointed like strange laser-beam guns of the future. I was queasy when I heard Mr. Cantor announce me, but I burst through the red velour as if this were the best moment of my life.

I caught a glimpse of myself on the monitor and saw someone else. Mr. Cantor and the other producers thought I was a comedian-singer-dancer-impressionist. And I was none of those.

"Who has more fun than a boy?" I sang. "I mean fun that is the real McCoy like football and baseball and swimming a lot."

Through sheer force of will, I made people believe that I was a song-and-dance man. I stole a little bit from a lot of my heroes, such as Jerry Lewis, Ray Bolger, and Danny Kaye. Flinging myself around the soundstage in Philadelphia was not too different from performing in our Cleveland living room for the relatives. "Joel, do something!" one of them would yell, and I would oblige, impersonating Aunt Estelle's ballet moves while Aunt Jean played the piano. I was not proficient as a singer, dancer, or comedian, but I was a very good faker and got away with it. Compared with pretending that I had feelings only for women and never, ever thought about men, this was a breeze.

After my whirling-dervish impression on his show, Mr. Cantor called me the "new Danny Kaye!" The televised reward for my performance was a phony spot in the cast of some future Broadway show—the real prize was an entrée, smoothed by Mr. Cantor, into the high-powered universe that was the William Morris Agency.

On my way to my first meeting at WMA's offices, I decided to walk up Broadway for inspiration. The marquees that glowed with the names of the day's biggest stars in theater—Lillian Hellman, Henry Fonda,

Helen Hayes, Mary Martin—reminded me of what all the nerves and worries were for. I passed Lindy's, where Milton Berle (also a WMA client) apparently ate almost every night. And although I couldn't have eaten a bite of cheesecake at that very moment—my stomach was so tied in knots—I imagined myself in one of the booths when I was rich and famous.

My interior pep talk fizzled out as soon as I arrived at the imposing skyscraper at 1740 Broadway, where WMA had its big, fancy offices. From the moment I stepped into the building's lobby with its dizzyingly high ceilings, I was overwhelmed. Businessmen clutching their briefcases and hats, secretary types in high heels, and delivery boys rapidly crisscrossed. I felt like I was the only one who didn't know where he was going.

I was ushered into a large conference room, where a parade of men from many departments came in to meet me and see what I was about. Everyone was dressed in a similar uniform of dark suits, white shirts, black ties, and black shoes, and I couldn't distinguish among them. In the conference room filled with suits, the Morris Men began their calculations.

"So you think you'd like to be on the stage, huh?" one said.

"What about movies?" another said.

"I say, we put him in nightclubs."

"He'll need an act."

"Somebody'll need to talk to the writing department."

"We can break in at a midnight audition at the Copa."

"I'll make a call."

Having decided my fate, the group quickly disbanded while I was still catching up. I had never considered becoming a nightclub performer. I had hardly been to any nightclubs in my eighteen years. But who was I to say no? The fact that WMA heavyweights were interested in me for anything was *big*. This was the agency that repped Marilyn Monroe, Judy Garland, Mickey Rooney, Danny Kaye, and Laurence Olivier! I was lucky that they had even let me walk into the office.

I practically sailed back to my hotel room with the feeling, "My God! I was on my way." As for nightclubs, the Copacabana was it. There was nothing bigger. Jerry Lewis and Dean Martin had debuted their comedy act at the famed hot spot on East 60th Street, which was owned partly by the notorious mob boss Frank Costello. When the time came for me to have my audition, failure was not an option, but it seemed the only one I had. I was about to go on the midnight show, unbilled, in the top nightclub in the world, and I had no idea what I was doing.

In my dressing room, I put on my tuxedo with shaky hands. After I fixed my bow tie, I reluctantly made my way to the club's kitchen, through which all the entertainers passed on their way to the small stage. Amid the steam rising up from the dishwasher's sink and the orders barked by line cooks, the Copa Girls entered in matching fruited turbans. Having just performed their number, they flashed by me, all flesh, fishnet stockings, perfume, and feathers.

"You're cute," one of them said to me.

"How old are you, anyway?" another laughed.

"Aw, leave the kid alone," a third said.

In a trail of giggles, they left me petrified. If the Copa Girls thought I was just some kid, what were the patrons, who had paid a lot of money to be there, going to think? I had got away with a lot in my short life, but I didn't know how I was going to manage this one.

I walked out into the dark near the dance floor, which doubled as a stage, where the Copa Girls had left an empty spotlight for me to die in. (There's nothing like being a short Jewish kid following a bouncy number by girls in sequined bustiers and mink panties.) I felt faintly claustrophobic in the tight space. There was a large, fake palm tree above, an orchestra behind, and squeezed all around the stage were tables of people drinking, smoking, eating, and laughing.

The atmosphere was so different from the austerely beautiful Play House and the seriousness of the theater. Though *Borscht Capades* was a revue with its share of shtick and humor, the theaters themselves in which we performed lent the show a sense of legitimacy. The Copa was a free-for-all. Even as the band struck up the opening chords for my act, the audience paid me about as much attention as they did the waiters rushing around the tables (actually, they paid those guys a lot more attention, since they were the ones serving the drinks). While I was performing, they laughed and talked, tucked into their Pu Pu platters (although the club was Latin-themed, it served Polynesian food), and smoked. My God, how they smoked! My eyes and throat burned with the stuff as I tried to ignore the talking and clinking of glasses and cutlery while singing my opener, "I'm Gonna Live Till I Die," which had been a big hit for Frank Sinatra. Throughout the patter, I had no idea whether I was bombing or killing it; the audience seemed so distracted.

"They loved you," George Wood, the legendary WMA agent, said as I came off.

Mr. Wood repped Sinatra. He also had many ties to the mob, including the Genovese crime family member Vincent "Jimmy Blue Eyes" Alo, who not only set up the casinos in Florida and Cuba with Meyer Lansky but was also the best man at Wood's wedding.

"You did great," he said. "Now go home and pack. We're going to Chicago."

"What? When?"

"In the morning."

My first 8 x 10 glossy, by the famous Chicago photographer
Maurice Seymour.

CHAPTER FIVE

My four-week engagement at The Chez Parée was first class all the way. It started with the club itself, which was quite a coup for me to be booked into right out of the gate. The Chicago venue hosted all the biggest names of the fifties, such as Frank Sinatra, Ethel Merman, Milton Berle, Jimmy Durante, Louis Armstrong, and Nat King Cole. Jack Eigen, the "midnight spieler" who had a long late-night radio career interviewing celebrities, broadcast from the lounge for years. The Chez Parée was the place to be seen, especially if you were a gangster—and in Chicago in the fifties, there were a lot of gangsters. Every night, big-time mobsters and their tootsies dressed to the nines populated the swanky joint.

I stayed at the Croydon Hotel, where all the road bands and touring actors (not the stars) stayed. The hotel's Circle Lounge provided the perfect meeting ground for vaudeville, cabaret, and theater performers looking to blow off some steam after a show. Oscar Peterson could often be found improvising on the piano, and the bandleader Harry James apparently proposed to Betty Grable at the big circular bar where I had my first grasshopper. I was practically on the floor after one of the sweet, bright green cocktails—I've never been a good drinker—but I wanted to fit in. Having a drink after the show is what a performer does; I was simply acting the part.

I didn't spend too much time in the Circle Lounge, since the job was pretty exhausting. I did two shows a night (the midnight show didn't get out until 2:00 A.M.) and in addition hung out with the high rollers who had asked to meet me. After a show, I'd go to their table to listen to their boring stories and smile as if they were charming and funny. Socializing went with the job.

As I went on, The Chez Parée's six hundred or so guests were just tucking into their dinners. I had to really work to compete with those rib eyes. My act was unusual for the nightclub circuit, where people out on the town for entertainment expected off-color material. Raunchy stories and blue language, however, didn't sound right coming out of a nineteen-year-old's mouth. It would have been like seeing one of their own kids talking dirty. So creating an act for me had been a challenge. But William Morris had enlisted its stable of comedy writers, who produced material for Danny Thomas, Danny Kaye, and its other top clients. The agency had also paid a lot of money for personalized orchestrations of the popular songs in my act.

The lyricist Ray Gilbert suggested I open with his Oscar-winning song, "Zip-a-Dee-Doo-Dah" from Disney's *Song of the South*, which I did. Ray is also responsible for giving me my name, Joel Grey. It had initially morphed from Joel Katz to Joel Kaye when I was announced on Eddie Cantor's TV show. About six months after I began on the nightclub circuit, however, it became clear that Joel Kaye was too close to Danny Kaye to be good for business. I was working with Ray to create new material for my act when I got a call from William Morris saying that if I was going to change my name I had to do it that day, since the marquee for my next engagement was going up tomorrow. Ray, ever the improviser, came out with, "Olé! Joel Grey!" adding, "The two *e*'s will look good up on the marquee." And like that, I became Joel Grey.

Jerry Seelen wrote me a piece of material called "Do You Remember?" The joke was that because I was so young, the "good old days" were last year. I brought up current events as if they were ancient history. Woven into the songs were impressions I did of the big stars of the day. I imitated Margaret O'Brien, the Shirley Temple of my generation, by crying, "Oh, Mr. Pasternak." (Joe Pasternak was a producer at MGM, and she was a big on-screen crier.) I also did an impression of Carmen Miranda that came out of one of my sessions with Ray. He worked closely with the Brazilian star, and at his house in LA, he had one of her turbans, which I decided to try on one day while we were working. With a pile of fruit on top of my head, I sambaed through his living room, trilling, "Tico-tico-tico." Ray roared at the sight of a young Jewish kid playing a Latin lady samba singer, and so did the audiences in the clubs. I finished "Do You Remember?" by saluting "a newcomer," and then I did my best Eddie Cantor, a classic show business old-timer, singing "If You Knew Susie." It was a good finish.

Toward the end of my act, when you usually do your strongest material, the club got very, very noisy, because the waitstaff were clearing all the plates before the main act. In this case it was Jane Froman, a *Ziegfeld Follies* alum and one of the biggest recording artists of the day. I was intimidated by Ms. Froman because of her fame and the sadness of her story. Her life was so dramatic that it had been turned into a movie—*With a Song in My Heart*, starring Susan Hayward. In 1943, a USO plane in which she had been traveling crashed, leaving her permanently disabled and confined to a wheelchair. As I came off, she was sweet and complimentary. "Sounded like a great audience," she said.

"They are just waiting for you," I replied before she wheeled onto the stage.

Ms. Froman was being kind, but my act *was* successful. The rare sight of a nineteen-year-old kid working the club scene got a lot of press. My smart innocence in a place typically filled with dark and dirty humor was the charm of it. Everybody in the room felt as if they were discovering me.

That included the Chez Parée Adorables, the club's showgirls who warmed up the crowd while wearing very, very little. Some did uncomplicated steps while others just stood around for decoration. All of them had great figures and weren't at all shy about showing them off. Passing by the dressing room where they got ready, I saw more bare breasts than I had ever seen in my life. If they knew I was looking (and who wouldn't look), they didn't seem to mind.

I caught the attention of an Adorable, one of the shorter girls who danced in the chorus and who were known as the "ponies." She was a little redheaded tap dancer named Missy, who showed no compunction in pursuing me. When I ran into her one night after the second show, it was almost as if she were waiting for me. Although I was always the passive participant when girls were drawn to me, I wasn't cool to their advances. Because I had been my mother's pet, having women fuss over me was something I was used to from an early age, and had almost come to expect. I knew my power and was excellent at playing the role expected of me. If Missy thought me a cocksman, I could do that as easily as ordering a grasshopper after the show.

I asked her out for a bite and a drink, glad to have the company. Over our late-night supper, I learned that she was from Canada and as excited as I to be making a buck as a performer. Missy wasn't particularly sophisticated or glamorous, but she sure was really cute and kind—and before I knew it, she was on the floor in my room and in my bed. Even if I wasn't especially interested in her, I felt pretty good about emulating the fabled life of a nightclub performer. A comedian and a showgirl, that happened all the time. And now it was happening to me. We slept together a number of times before I finished my engagement and returned home.

However, back in LA, two thousand miles away from the gig in Chicago, I got some perspective. I had a taste of the nightclub world and its money, girls, and travel, which were easy to get swept up in. But when I was honest with myself, I knew none of this was in the interest of my bigger dream of acting in the theater. Although they were both under the big umbrella of show business, a nightclub performer and theater actor were worlds apart.

While I was back home with Mom and Dad, I also learned that I had been accepted at UCLA. I had applied there during my senior year, while I was primarily traveling with *Borscht Capades*. My inspiration was Cousin Burton, who was already enrolled in UCLA. Burton and I were still close; he was straightforward and kind. And when I told him stories from the road, he was interested in the glamour but not so interested that it made me uncomfortable. Ours was an easy and trusting friendship.

My cousin and I had big plans. We were both going to pledge the Jewish fraternity, Zeta. I would study theater and be just another regular college kid on UCLA's idyllic campus. As I conjured up images from *Good News*, an MGM musical about college coeds, I found more and more to criticize about the nightclub circuit. I thought about the constant talking and clattering dishes while I was on. I couldn't say the audience was inattentive; there were guys trying to impress their dates, women getting drunk, couples making out. Some people thrived on the energy from a rowdy crowd and would be terrified to face the sea of quiet that marks the moment just before the start of a stage play, but I found the distractions disturbing. Part of the problem was that I was absolutely no good at ad-libbing, the stock-in-trade of nightclub performers. To be able to make something of the moment—a drunk in the crowd or a lady walking out to powder her nose—that's a special talent. Because I had been trained that it was unacceptable to say a line that was not in the play, improvising was verboten.

So I decided: I was going to UCLA. But before I had a chance to tell my parents, George Wood from William Morris called to say The Chez Parée wanted me back for another four weeks. When I told my parents about the call, they were so thrilled. I was confused by their excitement.

"I can't do that now," I said.

"Why not?" my mother blanched.

"I was accepted at UCLA. And I'm going."

I could see from their expressions how shocked they were.

"Son, you're grown up now," Dad said. "You have a career. You can't turn your back on this. School is a couple of years. You don't know if they will want you then. You have to strike while the iron is hot."

My father—who still kept busy doing the occasional tour as well as performances in LA, though he no longer enjoyed the success that comes with being brand new—couldn't fathom giving up a job that paid $500 a week to go back to school. A child of the Depression, he was fiercely practical.

"When you get out of college," he continued, "you're going to be looking for the job you have been offered right now."

I spent several days in total confusion. My position was supported by Burton and The Sisters, who probably wanted me to go to college because they knew how unhappy it would make my mother. Yet I could see my parents' point that this opportunity might not be there in four years. In the end, I decided to take the job and forget about college. It wasn't to make my parents happy. Still, when I arrived in Chicago I was really, really down. I mourned the loss of a deeper education. The last thing on my mind was Missy, but there she was when I returned, still kicking in the line. She surprised me by leaving a rose by my dressing table so that I knew we were still on. After opening that night, I took her out, and she had another surprise for me.

"I'm pregnant," she said.

"How did that happen?" I asked, in shock.

"You know how it happens."

"Are you sure?"

"Yes, I'm sure."

"So what do you want to do?"

"I want to have the baby."

"You're kidding."

"Why would I kid about something like that?" said Missy, who at this point was starting to get angry.

My mind raced. I liked Missy, but I barely knew her. I *didn't* know her.

"Is it mine?"

"Of course it's yours."

How could she be so sure? There was no reason to think she hadn't slept with someone else in the six weeks I was gone, but then again maybe it was mine. I couldn't believe what was happening. I didn't know what I was supposed to do or to whom I could talk. I couldn't tell my parents; that was for sure.

When I dropped Missy off at her place, she was crying, and I felt horrible. I hadn't said what she wanted to hear. I tried to console her by saying that we were both so tired we couldn't think straight and that everything would be clearer after we both got some rest. But it was just a stall tactic; I had absolutely no idea what was going to happen or how to deal with this.

Missy and I didn't talk the next day. When I saw her at the club, we just waved to each other. I didn't know what she was thinking, but maybe we could figure this thing out. Anyway, I had to get onstage, which was what I was being paid to do.

When I returned to my hotel after my second show, my time for procrastination was up. There in the lobby were two rough-looking men waiting for me. As soon as I walked in, they stood up from where they had been sitting and stepped in front of me.

"What's the problem?" I asked.

"You know the problem, and we're here to see that you make good."

Make good? What did that mean here? A ring for Missy? Or broken kneecaps for me? If I thought I was out of my depth before, now I was drowning. I felt as if I was going to faint. Instead, I darted around the thugs and ran up the steps to my room, where I locked the door. Then I called George Wood without a second thought about waking him up in the middle of the night. I told him everything and got scared when he said he didn't like any of it and that he was calling the owners of the Chez, Don Jo Medlevine and Dave "Dingy" Halper, immediately. If anyone knew his way around the mob, it was George.

But the next day Dingy and Don Jo told me to relax.

"If I had a nickel for every time I heard this story, I'd be rich," Don Jo said in their office the next day.

"You are rich!" Dingy said, laughing.

Don Jo began laughing, too, but they both stopped when they looked at me. I wasn't laughing; I felt like I was going to be sick. Never in a million years had I pictured myself running from gangsters and a girl—who might actually be pregnant.

"Look," Dingy said, putting a fatherly arm around my slumped shoulders. "It's not your kid—if there's a kid at all."

But for "insurance," I was accompanied by two big guys the bosses had hired for the rest of my time in Chicago. I was alone only when I was onstage. Missy and I avoided each other at the club. When the Adorables and I would pass one another to and from the stage, I would turn away so I wouldn't have to make eye contact. Whenever she would see me in the dressing room, she would look the other way.

I felt like a creep. I wanted to talk to Missy and deal directly with whatever was going on. But in the same passive way that I had responded to her advances, I went along with this mobster mentality. The fact is I acted like a selfish kid more than willing to avoid the consequences, whatever they might have been.

After I left Chicago, I never heard from her again.

My engagement at the Chez was just the start of what William Morris had planned to be the beginning of a big nightclub career. They booked me in spots all over the country: good ones, bad ones, and everything in between. Some were really bad, but they kept me working. Then they called in the spring of 1953 to say they'd succeeded in booking me at the London Palladium! This was a fantasy of every American performer. The theater played the best acts in Europe and the occasional American star, such as Judy Garland and Danny Kaye. Meanwhile I was going abroad for the very first time!

This was a *very* big opportunity with tremendous pressure to succeed, and I consequently developed a terrible case of laryngitis. Illness is the bane of a performer's existence. I always have a way of arriving at the worst possible moment—and my arrival at Heathrow *was* the worst moment for me.

Press agents from both the US and the UK had arranged for a gaggle of press to greet me as I came off the plane. The paparazzi blinded me with their large fan flashbulbs while reporters shouted.

"Look over here, Mr. Grey."

"No, over here, Joey."

"How do you like England?"

"Sing a few bars of something!"

My response: silence.

I couldn't utter a word, and even if I had, my thin, weak voice wouldn't have made a dent in the din. I was big news the next day. In my room at the Dorchester Hotel, where Danny Kaye always stayed, I read the tabloids, which all had variations of the same headline, PALLADIUM SINGER ARRIVES WITHOUT VOICE, accompanied by large, horrible pictures of me with a scarf wrapped around my neck and a look of agony in my eyes.

The press in England has always been a particularly vicious breed; they love anything that goes wrong. But luckily my laryngitis turned out to be a nonstory. Every day up until my debut, I saw a throat specialist on Harley Street who got me up and ready with a mix of gargles and meds.

I was one of a dozen acts that included a comedian, Jimmy Logan, who was a big name in Scotland; an acrobatic troupe; and an act called Vogelbein's Bears. (My dressing room was next to the bears'; back home, I got a lot of laughs when I said I shared a dressing room with dancing bears.) The headliner was Johnnie Ray, a big recording star who had just released a monster-hit song, "Cry." His single seemed to be the only thing playing on the radio.

Ray was a bobby socks idol. At the Palladium, the teenage girls swooned when he sang, "If your sweetheart sends a letter of goodbye / It's no secret you'll feel better if you cry." When he belted the last line, "So let your hair down and go right on baby and cry," the girls went so crazy that some of them threw their panties up on the stage. I discovered this because the stagehands hadn't completely swept the stage after his act one day. When I went on for the second show, I found myself dancing amid underwear of all shapes and sizes. While doing my Joel Grey faux ballet leaps during "Rumania," I improvised some steps to kick them out of the way.

Onstage, Ray brought to life the fantasies all these girls had while listening to his record. He flung himself around fearlessly, seemingly on the edge of losing control. Watching him was mesmerizing in the way that watching anything potentially perilous can be—he was like an accident just about to happen. He was a truly odd sex symbol—strange-looking to begin with, he wore a hearing aid, which in those days was not subtle. The apparatus had a wire that went down from his ear to his breast pocket.

Then there was the fact that he was gay.

Ray's homosexuality was a widely known open secret in the business. He had been arrested and pleaded guilty to having solicited men for sex in the restroom of a Detroit burlesque house in 1951, before the release of "Cry." Normally, the industry would have crucified him for being homosexual, but he made so many people so much money that it gave him some cover. Ray could take chances that I would never dare. Always petrified that anyone would think I was gay, I stayed far away from places or people that might get me in trouble.

Never had I imagined when I agreed to meet my first cousin once removed on Fanny's side that he would put me in that exact position. Cousin Louis's plan was to see the show and then afterward go out and have a drink. He told me to meet him at a pub on Jermyn Street, and as soon as I walked into the traditional pub with its wood-paneled wainscoting and leather seating, I spotted my cousin. I could see a family resemblance in the dark, pleasant-looking man dressed like a typical English businessman in a suit, tie, and shined shoes.

But there was something else about my cousin. There is a look among gay men, whether they are interested in one another or not. When I met Louis, I got it. I ordered a drink and, looking around, realized there were only men in the bar. It could have been a gentleman's club, but I knew better. The undercurrent of possibility was too strong. I wondered why my cousin had brought me here. I had never been to a place like this, not that I wasn't curious. Maybe he was testing me, because if I weren't homosexual I wouldn't get it. Either way, I felt instantly unsafe. If I were recognized in this place, and the press found out—even though it was all very innocent on my part (I was meeting a relative!)—that would have been it. I got through my one drink and then made an excuse about needing to call it a night in order to rest my voice.

If there was any part of me that wanted to stay in that bar, to see what goes on in a place like that, I didn't know it. I was filled with fear about all the bad things that could happen (and there were so many of them), and any possibility for desire was driven out. Riding in a black cab back to the hotel, I did, however, think about the lesson of Johnnie Ray: If you were going to be different, you had better be successful. Ever since I went on the road with *Borscht Capades,* I had this notion that achieving some level of fame could protect me from the kind of rejection I had experienced from my own mother after she discovered that I had had an affair with another man. I needed to succeed, and the best way for me to do that was on the stage.

The Palladium was a giant step in the right direction. After England, I reached a whole new level of prestige, and that meant booking lucrative engagements in Las Vegas. One of my first jobs was not in the new and flashy hotels such as the Flamingo, the Desert Inn, and the Sahara, but in the elegant El Rancho, which attracted a much more sophisticated crowd. The first casino resort built on the Strip, El Rancho was done in the style of a dude ranch but with Frette linens.

It was filled with West Coast society and celebrity types, such as those that went to the exclusive Racquet Club in Palm Springs. In Vegas, they came to gamble as well as be entertained and fed. El Rancho boasted the Chuck Wagon, the original all-you-can-eat buffet. Nobody had ever heard of such a thing in a hotel or nightclub. I ate there many nights, because if you were a performer, you were comped. El Rancho's headliners—such as Betty Grable, Chico Marx, Dorothy Dandridge, and Joe E. Lewis—played for the crowd in the Opera House where patrons dined on prime rib roasted in rock salt. My first time there I opened for Betty Garrett and Larry Parks. He was fresh off a success playing Al Jolson in *The Jolson Story*, which was a giant hit. Garrett was a well-known Broadway performer and married to Parks.

The owner of the hotel, Beldon Katleman, was very gruff but also very fond of me. Pleased with my work, he took me out for coffee and showed me around the hotel—and sent two women to my room. Gambling and girls go together. The high-end call girls at El Rancho blended perfectly with the guests. The two dark-haired beauties in elegant clothing that arrived at my hotel room door were no exception. When I saw them after opening the door, I naturally assumed they had to be some mistake.

"I'm sorry; I think you have the wrong room."

"You're Joel Grey, right?" the woman in the form-fitting jersey dress said.

"Yes."

"Mr. Katleman sent us."

"We're your birthday present," added the other woman with heavily applied black cat-eye makeup.

"It's not my birthday," I said like a dope.

They laughed and walked right in.

Sex was part of every aspect of Vegas, especially its entertainment. When I was booked the second time around at El Rancho, I was to open for Lili St. Cyr, the sexy and famous stripper. She was striking with her platinum-blonde hair, strong cheekbones, full lips, and arched black brows over heavy-lidded eyes. Of course, few people were looking at her face. Ms. St. Cyr's performance consisted of her removing her clothes in such unusual ways that she named a few of her acts "The Wolf Woman" and "The Chinese Virgin."

For her El Rancho engagement, she took a bath onstage. She came out with a beautiful robe, and someone helped her into an elegant tub, which sat atop a pedestal. To introduce her, I asked Ray Gilbert to write something special. So when I finished my act, I came back onstage, all sweaty, after my bow. The lights dimmed and I introduced Lili St. Cyr with this poem (said with a very straight face):

> *I wish I was the stopper*
> *That's inside Lili's tub*
> *When she gets in to take a bath*
> *Glub, glub, glub . . . glub . . . glub!*

Late at night, when the second shows at each resort and casino were over, a lot of the acts, hyped up and not ready for bed, would gather. Besides hanging out (most of us were ravenous since we hadn't eaten before our shows) at the Chuck Wagon or other restaurants, we would also check out other lounge acts such as the Treniers, Louis Prima and Keely Smith, who regularly held forth until five o'clock in the morning. That's when the acts would cool down before walking outside to the sun coming up in 100-degree weather. Sometimes we would head back to the Chuck Wagon for breakfast (before sleeping until three in the afternoon).

In the moody and loose atmosphere of the lounges along the Strip, performers connected. That's how Harry Belafonte became a good friend. We had both been bitten by the theater bug early in life. Like my experience with the Cleveland Play House, all it took was one show at the American Negro Theater to set him on his life's path. He had been working as a janitor's assistant in the forties when a tenant gave him a ticket to the legendary Harlem theater. His musical career singing in nightclubs was just a way for him to make money for acting classes. Serious about the craft, he participated in the New School's Dramatic Workshop program where Marlon Brando, Bea Arthur, Tony Curtis, and Harry's friend Sidney Poitier were also students. But his recording success happened first and got in the way of his acting, a dilemma I, too, knew something about.

There was a significant difference between Harry and me. Las Vegas during that time was virulently racist, and Jim Crow laws were strictly enforced at the new clubs and restaurants along the strip. Even the top black entertainers of the day, such as Louis Armstrong, Nat King Cole, and Ella Fitzgerald, had to enter venues through stage or kitchen doors and stay in boardinghouses in the poor black area called Westside. When Sammy Davis Jr. went swimming at the New Frontier, the manager drained the "whites only" pool afterward.

It was hard to find restaurants where Harry and I could eat together. But when we did, we had great times talking about theater, music, girls. A few years later, we shared a bill at Bill Miller's Riviera in Fort Lee, New Jersey. Harry had already released his album *Calypso*, which sold more than a million copies. I could barely get on after he sang "Day-O." It was a sexy, thrilling performance, and it took about ten minutes for the audience to get him and that song out of their heads. After that engagement, I ordered a gold medallion engraved with TO HARRY, MAZEL! LOVE, JOEL as a closing gift to mark a successful engagement. But when it arrived, it read TO HARRY MAZEL. LOVE, JOEL. He's worn it ever since.

Perhaps the most unusual friendship I made from my time in Las Vegas, however, was with another legendary stripper, Sherry Britton. Like Lili St. Cyr, Ms. Britton put her own twist on the art of taking her clothes off. One of her signature features (other than her hourglass figure) was her long, jet-black hair. When she wore it in front, it draped over her breasts; when she pushed it back, it covered her behind.

I met Sherry in Vegas during an engagement at the Desert Inn, and we hit it off instantly during one of those after-hours hang-outs. Sherry was truly stunning, funny, and smart—and Jewish! Like Gypsy Rose Lee, Sherry wasn't just a bimbo who took her clothes off for money. The one-liners ("I strip, but I don't tease") rolled off her tongue effortlessly; this was a stripper who read the classics during her off hours. She brought intelligence and class to her act, removing elegant evening gowns of chiffon to the equally delicate music of Tchaikovsky.

Sherry was quite the sensation in Las Vegas with a long list of suitors that included many high rollers and members of the mob. After watching my show, she was effusive as well as affectionate. Of course, I laid on the charm as thickly as I could. I was impressed with her. She was tiny—even shorter than I—but onstage, she looked like an Amazon. Sherry was a goddess out there. I also liked how sought-after she was. When it came to flirting, she set the rules. But I could make her laugh, and she went for that. I felt something happening between us, and before anyone even had a chance to think about it, we were a couple.

There was real chemistry between us. You would have to be dead not to be turned on by Sherry. Her body was legendary, even among the jaded audiences of Las Vegas, who had seen an untold number of women take it almost all off. Any doubts I had about myself vanished when we were together. The sex was very exciting and powerful, and it felt right. It began with the fact that we really liked each other and had a lot to talk about. She was extremely literate and loved the theater. Given her profession, her erudition was delightfully surprising, and the fact that she was a Jewish stripper always made me chuckle. There was probably something to the fact that it doesn't get more hetero than dating a stripper, and not just any stripper, a world-famous stripper. But at the time, my connection with Sherry didn't feel as if I was trying to prove to myself that I was straight. It just felt right!

Of course, it didn't hurt that with Sherry on my arm, my reputation instantly soared. I became known as some kind of a stud and was the envy of every man on her long list of her admirers. I knew they were all wondering, *What's he got?* It was a fair question. Fourteen years older than I, she enjoyed a younger lover on his way to the big time (at least according to the local gossip columns). As a couple out in public—she the sophisticated older woman and I the energetic up-and-comer—we got a lot of attention. (At one point a gossip columnist in LA printed an item that we were on our way to the altar. In Vegas, that can happen in a second, and I got a panicked call from my dad, and I could hear Mother next to him.)

When my Vegas engagement ended, I flew back to New York, and Sherry joined me a couple of weeks later. We were going out to the theater, clubs, etc., and usually ending up at my place, on 57th Street at First Avenue. Not too long after, though, I found out that she had been in a longtime relationship with a much older man in New York and was still seeing him. I don't know which of us was the guy on the side, but without any strain Sherry and I both took up with our previous lives. (I could hear the sigh of relief from Mickey and Grace all the way from LA.) There were never hard feelings between Sherry and me, and we stayed friends for years.

New York might not have had the high-thread-count sheets of Vegas suites, but it did have the theater. I went to every Broadway show, where I saw many legendary performances, such as Lee J. Cobb in *Death of a Salesman*, Mary Martin in *South Pacific*, and Yul Brynner in *The King and I*. Each of them inspired and depressed me at the same time. Those shows were thrilling, the acting magnificent, but though I wanted it desperately, I didn't have a place in that world, and whatever success or name I had made thus far did not make the crossover in any way easier.

But I kept trying. I read *Variety* and *Backstage* from cover to cover; hung out at the Gray drugstore in the Theater District hoping I might hear about a promising audition; and bugged the William Morris agents in the theater department. I did everything I could think of, but legitimate theater producers and directors thought of me only as a nightclub comic. They feared that people like me from the "variety" world would sully the high-minded idea of the theater as a place of art.

Ironically, it was my father who called me in the summer of 1951 to offer me my first part on Broadway. Although *Borscht Capades* wasn't as popular as it once was, it continued to play around the country and in Los Angeles. Its core audience was always going to be there for it, which was the rationale for my father's latest plan. He was taking *Borscht Capades* to the Great White Way—and he wanted me to be the show's Juvenile Star. My heart sank. I needed to break out of the stereotype of a song-and-dance man, not advertise it in the heart of the Theater District.

"Dad, this is big," I said. "Believe me, I know this is a big thing, for you. And I have a really good feeling in my bones about it. But it's not the right thing for *me*."

"I understand . . ."

"I'm sorry, Dad."

"No, no, no. I can see where you're coming from."

"I hate to disappoint you."

"No, sweetheart. I had to ask. But I'm sure you're right."

As horrible as it was to say no to my own father, he did understand. Even though he was thrilled with my nightclub career, he had long sensed my unhappiness with it. Not every gig was El Rancho. Not long before Dad asked me to join him in *Borscht Capades* on Broadway, I played the Town Casino, a massive club in Buffalo with all the charm of a warehouse. It was the dead of winter and nobody was going out, which explained why there were maybe ten audience members in a place that held 350. After I finished my opening number, "Zip-a-Dee-Doo-Dah," a guy ringside who was feeling up his girlfriend turned around and yelled at me, "Get off the stage. Nobody wants to see you, anyway." Respect and attention were rare in nightclubs, no matter who was onstage; it was just not that kind of an atmosphere. People came to show off and be outrageous, not listen. I finished the show, which I had been paid to do. But when my father met me at the airport in LA (accompanied by my mother and Grandma Fanny, who had brought along a thermos of her barley soup, because she was sure nobody else had fed me), I was sure I couldn't go on doing the clubs.

Dad asked me to join *Borscht Capades* simply because he knew I would enhance the show, and he loved for us to be together, which made my decision not to do it even more difficult. Hal Zeiger, however, was a little less forgiving, calling me an "ungrateful little shit."

Hal's comment stung, because of course I felt like an ungrateful little shit. What kind of son was I to hold out on the father who had come to my rescue and shown me unconditional love when I was at my lowest moment, after the cantor? Not to mention that he'd launched my career by having given me a part in his show. Eddie Cantor, William Morris: none of that would have happened without *Borscht Capades*. The guilt only worsened when the show struggled as soon as it arrived on Broadway. Finally, it became too much, and I agreed to come in for a few weeks to help. But it was too late; *Borscht Capades* closed less than three months after it opened.

Dad lost $35,000 and returned to Los Angeles to start all over again. When a bill for an additional $5,000 from the IRS arrived, he had to sell the house on Malcolm Avenue to pay it. Witnessing my father with nothing, after he'd experienced the biggest success of his life with his brilliant comedy records and live show, made me worry about the career to which I was committing myself. But when William Morris called with the next job, another stint at El Rancho, I took it. And when I received that much-needed paycheck, I happily sent Dad a thousand dollars.

"The only suggestion of the appeal," the *New York Times* critic wrote, "lies in the galvanized miming of a pint-sized newcomer named Joel Grey."

CHAPTER SIX

was seated in my dressing room in my underwear and still-damp tuxedo shirt after the second show of my act, which I was doing at the Mocambo—the so-of-the-moment nightclub on Sunset Boulevard where the stars (Ava Gardner, Betty Grable, Artie Shaw, and Frank Sinatra) gamboled—when the owner, Charlie Morrison, stuck his head in and announced, "Miss Lana Turner would love for you to join her at her table."

Smiling at my dumbstruck expression, he added, "So get dressed quickly, young star, and follow me."

Of course, I knew Lana Turner was in the audience; I saw her ringside the minute I stepped onstage for the late show. I nearly forgot the first lines of my opening song, "The More I See You."

The more I see you, the more I want you.
Somehow this feeling, just grows and grows

Next to Rita Hayworth, who was so unbelievably sexy in *Gilda*, Miss Turner was my absolute favorite movie star. Her historic ascent to stardom from sipping a soda at the fountain of Schwab's Pharmacy nearby on Sunset Boulevard was big-time LA lore (she was actually at the Top Hat Malt Shop—but what did that matter?). To my astonishment, she was even more beautiful in person. Luckily, by my third number I was able to restore my professionalism and do one of my better shows, but I remained nervous the entire time.

Now with Mr. Morrison staring at me in my underwear, I realized I had to get moving—towel-off quickly, remove what was left of the pancake, and, oh, yes . . . . put on some pants!

"You were just wonderful," Miss Turner, up close and personal, said to me. Not only was the actress beautiful, but she smelled amazing, too. "Where do you get all that energy? And so late at night?"

Gulp

"I dedicated my show to you."

I hardly noticed that she was sitting with a woman friend until Miss Turner introduced us, adding, "We're going to my place just up the hill for a nightcap. Would you like to join us?"

Oh, Mommy, would I?

I struggled to get the words out: "That sounds very nice."

That sounds so lame, Joel.

Her limo was parked outside, and it was agreed that I'd follow them up the hill in my little VW to her house, which, I'd read in *House & Garden*, was one of the best examples of classic California architecture. Out the big windows overlooking Los Angeles, the city lights seemed to shine all the way west to the Pacific Ocean.

Her butler greeted us with a tray of three glass flutes, but the excellent pink champagne didn't relax me any. Miss Turner, rumored to have many lovers, particularly favored powerful men, not only in show business—but also, reportedly, in the mob. Seated in her living room, I kept picturing some ruthless gangster storming in to find me sipping champagne with his moll at this unwholesome hour.

After finishing my drink, I looked at my watch (as if I didn't already know the time) and began apologizing for the hour. "I had no idea how late it was," I said. "Excuse me; I have two shows tomorrow night. This was so nice of you. You have a wonderful place. Thank you for coming to my show." I was talking very, very fast and was out the door even faster. I'll never know where that evening with Miss Tuner could have gone, but driving home I got to thinking that Glenn Ford was unbelievably sexy in *Gilda*, too.

As it turned out, on the same night that Lana Turner had come to the Mocambo, a table of producers and casting agents from Warner Bros. also were checking me out—and would later offer me my first movie role.

About Face, set in a Southern military school, centered on the lives of cadets bending and breaking the rules during their senior year. The film, a musical-comedy remake of *Brother Rat*, starred Gordon MacRae, Eddie Bracken, and Dick Wesson as the hotshot cadets—and I was cast as the lowly plebe Bender. "Finn out, Bender!" they were always barking at my pathetic character. I might have been playing a twerp, but I was going to be in the movies! I had never even auditioned for a film role before, and this one was offered to me without so much as a screen test. Ever since I had moved to Los Angeles, the movies had always been a fantasy. I felt important with a sticker on my car window that granted me access into the Warner Bros. lot, where I had stood as a kid with my autograph book. My favorite part of the job was the commissary, where I ate lunch right next to the Warner Bros. film players, a who's who of Hollywood.

There was no doubt that *About Face* was a good break. It was an amusing role, but I was the only cast member with no song, let alone dance number. All of the songs were written for the upperclassmen and their visiting girlfriends. My first movie musical and no music? I wondered, *What would Mickey Rooney do?*

I came up with my own number. Approaching the choreographer, LeRoy Prinz, I said, "What would happen if in the scene where Bender's told, 'Just remember, you're nobody' by one of the cadets, he replies, 'I'm nobody . . .'" I then launched into a comedic soliloquy of low self-esteem with a few Jerry Lewis imitations for good measure. (Everyone wanted to be Jerry Lewis back then.)

Mr. Prinz liked the idea a lot. He and I wrote and rehearsed "I'm Nobody" and then went to the head of the studio, who gave us a green light to go ahead and add it to *About Face*. Even though the movie was poorly received when it opened, in the spring of 1952 (the *New York Times* described it as "overstuffed with inane dialogue and feeble gags"), my performance got noticed. "The only suggestion of the appeal," the *Times* critic wrote, "lies in the galvanized miming of a pint-sized newcomer named Joel Grey . . . Mr. Grey rates a snappy salute in an entertainment package that deserves nothing more than an overripe raspberry."

Naturally, I was happy to be noticed in the *Times*, but generally the rule I've experienced through my career is that when a movie bombs, you might as well not be good in it. My cameo in *About Face* led to a few television parts, but I still couldn't seem to get hired in the theater, the only place I really wanted to be.

I spent a lot of time in the office of my splendid agent, Charlie Baker, head of the theater department at William Morris, being upset about parts I didn't get. And he always tried to cheer me up and on.

"There's no reason to beat yourself up," he said sympathetically. "They simply went a whole other way. C'mon, let's go to the Oak Room. I need a martini."

Charlie, whose clients included Angela Lansbury, Jack Lemmon, Walter Matthau, and Barbara Cook, was a true gentleman in an often sleazy business. The Harvard-educated World War II Navy lieutenant, well versed in the history of the theater, was elegant and effete to the point of being aristocratic. With his perfect martinis, clothes from J. Press, and country home in Sneden's Landing, Charlie was known for his taste. He also became a passionate advocate of mine. It was a coup and an honor having him believe in me. However, he seemed to be the only one certain I'd succeed.

My disappointments were many. I had desperately wanted to be in *No Time for Sergeants*, a play about a rube from the sticks and his misadventures as he's drafted into the Army during World War II. But they wouldn't see me. I went up for the part of Rolf, the young Nazi who is in love with Liesl in Richard Rodgers and Oscar Hammerstein's *The Sound of Music*. My rendition of "Sixteen Going on Seventeen" didn't make Mr. Rodgers's ears perk up any. Even when John Kander—a talented composer and close friend who was at the beginning of his career, accompanied me on the piano for my audition for a show called *Irma la Douce*—I still didn't get the part.

I had a couple of strikes against me when it came to getting work in the theater. First there was my nightclub act. Having a variety performer in your legitimate show could easily be perceived as déclassé. The other issue was anti-Semitism.

Charlie took me to a party, a seated dinner held at a swell address on the Upper East Side, where blue-blooded theater types engaged in intellectual exchanges about the latest shows. So I was stunned to hear "kike," the clipped sound of that ugly word, coming forcefully from the mouth of our prominent host. Even more surprising was my response: nothing. I said nothing. After I left the dinner and long after that, I continued beating myself up for not having said *something*.

Hiding or at least not announcing being Jewish was evidence of a deep conflict within me (although I was the son of the most Jewish performer in the business, theater people had no idea who Mickey Katz was). Denying yet another part of myself activated those feelings from childhood that there was something inherently wrong with me. It also finally persuaded me to listen to my agents' conviction that plastic surgery on my nose would lead to a broader variety of parts. I had fought the idea for a long time. It felt crummy that I had to change such a fundamental part of myself in order to be acceptable. Why was a turned-up Aryan nose better? The answer was a difficult one to face; the pressure to change my nose was about anti-Semitism, and I rightfully hated that idea. Yet I so wanted and needed to work that I went ahead with the surgery.

Of course, Mother was all for it, particularly since she had already had her nose done. In Los Angeles, where plastic surgery was beginning to flourish right along with the palm trees, Mother was one of the first to do it. (Just like with fashion or food, she was always one of the first.) Aunt Jeannie followed by a month, then Aunt Helen, Aunt Fritzi, Aunt Esther, and oh, yes, the baby, Beverly—all of them except Estelle. (Hmm, what did she know?!) They all had plastic surgery for the same reason they had followed us out to California—they didn't want Grace to have anything that they didn't. The whole family even went to the same surgeon!

So when I eventually gave in, Mother herself took me to her wonderful Dr. Jessie Fuchs. My entire face was swollen and bandaged after the operation, but Dr. Fuchs assured me that I would be pleased with his work when the swelling went down. It took a good six months for my nose to reveal an ordinary and perfectly generic shape, but in the end I did think it looked fine. More important, I hoped that my new, less ethnic nose could help my career.

Thinking back, I'm certain without the surgery I never would have got the plum part of Jack in NBC's 1956 telecast of an original musical version of *Jack and the Beanstalk*. With my hair bleached so blond that it was nearly white and my slightly swollen pug nose, I looked like the perfect non-ethnic fairy-tale character. Written by Helen Deutsch, hot after the success of the film *Lili*, starring Leslie Caron, *Jack and the Beanstalk* was an expensive, high-quality production.

The tension on the set right before we went live was high, and all the pressure fell on my shoulders. I was in every scene, singing and dancing. It didn't help that my understudy had clearly watched *All About Eve* one too many times. All during rehearsals, he kept looking for me to break my leg. I saw out of the corner of my eye, moments before going on air, his face with an incredulous expression that read, *How could you do this to me?*

No matter: All went off without a hitch, and it was a giant step. I got good notices. The William Morris crew thought *Jack and the Beanstalk* was going to jettison me into the big time. It didn't. It brought more television opportunities. The following year, I had a three-episode arc in *December Bride* as the fresh-faced, showbiz-crazy nephew of the sitcom's star Spring Byington, who was like an older Lucille Ball. Also in 1957, I played a teenage killer who beats up a woman and is on the verge of killing her child in a realistic and violent episode of Bell Telephone's *Telephone Time* drama series. With my face covered in mud and blood, it was exciting to work against type and play an aggressor, and I got to recover some of my acting chops. Much less enthusiastically, I took a role in the low-budget movie musical *Calypso Heat Wave*, in which I recycled dance steps I had made up for *About Face*. The only memorable thing about the movie was a cameo by Maya Angelou, then a little-known singer who had released a calypso album.

The fight to become an actor wasn't the only persistent battle in my life. Throughout my twenties, I continued to wage a sexual war with myself. No matter how many women I was sleeping with, my conflict with men was never *not* there. I told myself I was bisexual, because I was attracted to women and men. But if I really looked at it, I would have to admit that was because being gay was simply not an option.

Trying so hard to be what society, including my parents, insisted I *should* be was exhausting. Particularly because when I did have relationships with men I had to be extremely careful not to be discovered. During the year that Ted, a publicist, and I spent together in the mid-fifties, he often brought me home to his parents' house for Shabbos, and no one ever suspected we were anything more than business associates and friends. Over a delicious dinner at their gracious apartment at 80th Street and Riverside Drive, his lovely family didn't have a clue as to the true nature of our relationship. To them I was simply their son's client, a nice young Jewish boy living in New York away from his family. They took me in and made me feel like a part of theirs.

Ted wasn't my first hidden adult relationship with a man. Before him, there was Robby, whom I met while shopping at Bloomingdale's. I was looking for linens for the very first apartment I lived in alone—a one-bedroom at 400 East 57th Street with a sunken living room and cork floors that was all very Paul McCobb. While I was feeling the thread count of the sheets, Robby, an up-and-coming interior designer, offered me some advice. I knew instantly that he couldn't care less about linens. When secrecy is part of your life, you develop a heightened awareness to *the look*.

The look, a certain minuscule brightening, widening of the eyes, can't ever be denied or reversed. It can be nonsexual—a perfectly friendly hey-I-get-it acknowledgment. Or it can be angry, as in the defiant look, which says, *How dare you know a secret about me that I'll spend a lifetime denying.* But the best is the healthy admiring look and a smile that says, *Hey! We're from the same shtetl.*

Connecting with someone was a relief; I could be unguarded and myself. But because the connection was forbidden, it was also electric. Robby, an erstwhile Orthodox Jewish boy from Brooklyn, had gone on to marry a Boston Brahman, joining a group of well-known figures in the design field who had put aside their sexuality (either permanently or intermittently) for the sake of wives and children.

I liked Ted and Robby a lot, but I knew deep down that neither would figure in my future. (I parted undramatically with both and remained good friends.) I never allowed myself even to imagine such a life. My agent, Charlie Baker, was gay, but no one at the office or the high society in which he moved seemed to acknowledge that discreet aspect of him. I stayed many times in his place in Sneden's Landing, where some of the great theater people at the time had homes, but if he had lovers, I never met them.

And this was complicated by the fact that I wanted a family. I always knew this, from the time I was a little boy wandering around the Sovereign Hotel in Cleveland. Whenever there was an infant in the hotel, I had to stop and stare. The Davises, a couple who lived on our floor, couldn't help noticing my interest in their baby and asked if I would like to hold her. Oh, yes, I would! I turned out to be very good at it, and Mrs. Davis let me give her six-month-old a bottle while she watched. I wound up babysitting little Nicole while her mother did other things; I loved holding, burping, and even diapering her. I knew right then that one day I'd be a dad.

Robert Anderson's 1953 Broadway hit *Tea and Sympathy,* about a man who resolves his conflicted sexuality with a compassionate woman, had a profound impact on me. Directed by Elia Kazan and starring Deborah Kerr, making a remarkable Broadway debut, and a young John Kerr (no relation), the play centered on a seventeen-year-old, Tom, who is bullied by his prep school classmates because they assume his lack of ability with sports and girls means he's a queer. Tom is drawn to the beautiful and sympathetic headmaster's wife, played by Ms. Kerr, who in an act of unselfish generosity ends up validating him by taking him to her bed. In the quiet after making love, she says to Tom, "When you talk of this in years to come, and you will, be kind." Broadway was shocked by this scene and the ideas the play dealt with so frankly, but I was inspired. I identified wholeheartedly with Tom during this confusing time. No matter how I conducted my personal life, becoming a husband and dad was my biggest desire, just as important as making it in the theater or becoming famous.

The only problem was that I was twenty-six years old and still single. That might not have seemed that old, even at that time, but I felt that it was. Many of my straight friends wed by twenty-one or twenty-two and were already on their second child. My primary example, my parents, married when they were seventeen and nineteen. Even Ronnie, my little brother, whom I had always dismissed as a baby, had a wonderful wife.

Ron took the path I hadn't chosen: He went to UCLA, where he was Zeta Beta Tau and met Maddie, a nice Jewish girl from the sister sorority. They were immediate soul mates. Ronnie and I never had a lot in common and didn't have a close relationship. Mother didn't help by always showing her strong bond with me, the one who might make her famous. Growing up, the poor kid had to sit in the theater night after night watching everyone fall all over me during my performances in *Borscht Capades.* Meanwhile, I saw him as someone who was interested only in business.

Once he got married, however, everything changed. I instantly loved Maddie, who was so giving and easy and optimistic and gentle. She and I became like brother and sister (we always called each other that), and in turn Ronnie and I grew much closer. Maddie, the complete opposite of our mother, helped ease whatever competition our mother had stoked between us so that we could just enjoy each other. (Mother, not quite as big a fan of Maddie's as the rest of us, took every opportunity to give her daughter-in-law helpful suggestions, such as "You shouldn't wear that dress, dear. It makes your legs look even shorter than they are.") Mother might not have loved her, but I was happy in their LA home and even more so when soon after their wedding they told me that Maddie was expecting.

With my younger brother doing everything I was unable to do, I started to feel old and self-conscious. Yet I couldn't seem to stay on the straight and narrow.

There were nights when I went out of my way to pass the infamous Everard Baths, wondering what was happening behind the nineteenth-century limestone walls of the building on West 28th Street. What was I missing? Hidden from sight, I watched who went into the gay bathhouse (nicknamed "Ever-*hard*"). I desperately wanted to go in, but I was also deeply afraid.

This was the fifties, and a vehement crackdown on men having sex with men was well under way. President Dwight D. Eisenhower issued an executive order, formalizing policy that had begun during Truman's administration, which denied federal government security clearances to people because of their sexual orientation. The FBI conducted surveillance of gays and harassed them; the police continued to raid gay bars, hauling off well-dressed businessmen in handcuffs for photographers to capture, their families to see, and their lives to be ruined.

Even though I knew all of this, the arched entryway of the Everard proved too exciting to ignore. One night, feeling that *I have to do this*, I walked in just like a regular and paid my entrance fee. With an equal mix of fear and anticipation I took my key and towel from the clerk.

I was still in the locker room, totally naked, my towel over my shoulder and with no idea what awaited me, when I felt a poke on my shoulder and then heard someone say, a little too loudly, "Joel Grey. What are *you* doing here?"

I can't remember what happened after that. The next thing I knew I was hailing a cab on Lexington and begging the driver to step on it. It takes a lot for me to cry, but it was all I could do when I got home that night. Beating myself up for wanting something that had the capacity to destroy me, I cried and cried. At some point I stopped, washed my face, got into bed, and tried to forget the whole thing.

This woman is a beauty, I thought.

CHAPTER SEVEN

moved through the fine mid-century modern furniture, just looking, not looking to buy—I didn't need anything. A viewing for an estate sale at an auction house on the corner of Wilshire and La Cienega was always amusing. And, of course, you never know.

"Joel!"

I was looking up from an Arne Jacobsen chair I was trying out; it was Dan, one of my William Morris agents, and on his arm was a striking girl with dark brown hair tied up in a knot.

"Jo, you gotta meet this kid," Dan said to his date, who turned her dark almond eyes on me. "He sings; he dances! The office is really high on him."

At twenty-nine, I was hardly a kid, but I was more interested in this woman than in correcting him. There was something unusual about her beauty—high cheekbones and sexy buckteeth like Gene Tierney's—that made me think I had seen her before.

After Dan gave me the trademark William Morris agent hug (performed while scanning the room to see who else was there), he introduced her to me: "Jo, I'd like you to meet Joel Grey. The office thinks he is going to do big things. Joel, this is Jo Wilder, an actress we just signed from New York."

Jo Wilder? Something *was* familiar.

"Been in LA long?" I asked her.

"No," she said. "I've just come out."

"Oh? Where in the city do you live?"

"On Lafayette, across from the Public."

Then it hit me.

"You're June Ericson's roommate! We've met!"

The singer June Ericson was the girlfriend of Peter Matz (a successful composer for film, theater, and TV—and my good friend from Hami High). She was also one of three women who had shared a cool loft—before lofts were lofts—in the Colonnade, a landmark building on Lafayette right across the street from the Public Theater. (The third roommate was Charlotte Foley, who went on to originate the role of Electra, the stripper, in the Ethel Merman production of *Gypsy*.) About a year earlier, I had gone there one night with Peter to pick up June and met Jo quickly. The introduction clearly hadn't made an impression on either of us.

Now, in the auction house, something was going on between us. She looked different to me. *This woman is a beauty*, I thought. An odd mix of feisty, vulnerable, and sexy, she had a presence. Even though she appeared to be Dan's date, there was no doubt that something was sparking. While Dan was busy, she wrote her number on a Du-par's matchbook and handed it to me. I guess she *wasn't* Dan's girl after all.

I couldn't stop thinking about her that night—or for the next few days. I was living in LA for TV pilot season. "You gotta be here," my agent said, because the bluebird of happiness (aka big money and security) was a TV series. Although I made several pilots throughout my career that didn't sell, I never stopped pursuing that bird. So I always maintained a presence in the form of an apartment on the West Coast and would go back and forth between New York and LA.

Finally I pulled out the Du-par's matchbook and called Jo. Why was

I so nervous? After a couple of minutes of small talk I said, "I'm invited to a party at the top of Laurel Canyon tonight. There'll be people from the business. It's a great house, and they're great pals." She didn't wait a second to say, "Yes, I'd love to." I was shocked by how excited her answer made me.

Just as we had planned on the phone, I arrived late that afternoon at the apartment she shared with three girls, walked up the steps, and rang the bell. The door opened, and there was some other girl.

"I'm here for Jo," I said. "Can you tell her I'm here?"

"Are you sure? She's not home."

Thinking she must just be running late, I asked, "Do you mind if I come in and wait? It must be 900 degrees out here."

"Sure, come on in," the roommate said before she went into what I assumed was her bedroom and shut the door. Looking hard at my watch, I was sure I specified six o'clock. Thumbing through a *Photoplay* magazine, I managed to kill ten minutes. After a half hour went by, my annoyance slowly turned into anger, and by seven o'clock I slammed down the magazine before slamming the apartment door. I had been stood up!

I gunned my little Fiat up the winding canyon, driving much too fast, and arrived at my friends' house shaking with anger. The host tried to calm me down, but, humiliated, I didn't want any of it. "Maybe something was wrong," he said. "Maybe she got ill. Who knows what. Why don't you at least call her?"

After a vodka gimlet, I dialed her number. She picked up.

"Jo?"

"Oh, Joel. Sorry. *We* were at the beach and then got stuck in bad traffic on Sunset."

Silence.

"But I'm here, and I'm ready!"

Silence.

Ready? I was ready, too. Ready to hang up, which I did. To think that I would just turn around and come get her! My overreaction was a sign that I was really attracted to her. But it also stemmed from my larger frustration in constantly looking for a woman with whom I could share my life. Even though I had had relationships with men, I never fully committed to any of them—let alone the idea of being with a man long term. I always dated women in the hope of finding the one who could be a wife and mother. That was never out of mind. Even to the point of spoiling some of my pursuits with guys.

So maybe some of my anger was misplaced. In fact, when Jo called a couple of days later, I was still pissed. That's how interested I was. On the phone, she never stopped talking: Portia pleading her case, begging for that "quality of mercy." She needn't have; since she stood me up I hadn't been able to think about much else other than her. I agreed to take her to dinner.

I took her to a little southern-Italian restaurant, cuisine that was just becoming a trend in the Valley. Having never seen anything like the red-and-white-checkered tablecloths and dripping candles in Chianti bottles, we were charmed. Over dinner we discovered we knew a lot of the same people in New York, and had a great deal in common. For sure we were both besotted with the theater and passionate about music and liberal politics (some of her relatives, she told me, were communists). We had both been ballet students; we both wanted to sing. (She was a gifted singer, and I had no idea what I was doing, but I was working on it—hence my voice lessons three times a week.) We had both changed our names and our noses. And, oh, yes, we were both Jewish.

Jo had been born Joan Carrie Brower to Clara and Izzy Brower of Brownsville, Brooklyn. In the infamous, rough neighborhood where they lived, an enclave of Central European Jews, Izzy was a pharmacist. Clara also got a degree in pharmaceutical science, impressive and unusual for a woman at the time, though she never ended up practicing. She found she could not cope and spent pretty much the rest of her life in bed with a mysterious back ailment.

The Browers—including her grandmother, who lived upstairs with her second husband, a rabbi—were always extremely critical of Jo's desire to be an actress, and they did everything they could to stand in her way. Her older brother Mitchel, who was also interested in the theater, was sympathetic and her ally. She was forever upset that her family didn't understand or truly see her for who she was, which I could relate to. So she distanced herself from them by moving to Manhattan to make a whole new life. One of her big breaks was replacing Jo Sullivan, the original Polly Peachum, early in the run of the historic production of Brecht-Weill's *Threepenny Opera* at the Theater de Lys. I was impressed that something so edgy and arty was part of her résumé.

The conversation didn't falter for a second. I made her laugh so much that she had to beg me to stop—otherwise, she said, she would wet her pants. I already felt the desire to make up for her unhappy family life.

After dinner, we went back to my apartment in West Hollywood. From the small terrace above the strip that I filled with plants, the lights of LA were far-reaching and magical. I was attracted to her, and we felt so connected in that moment, I thought, *She could be the one.* Although there was a high level of sexual excitement between us, the idea that this, that *we*, could work was not simply sexual. It was about compatibility. In this beautiful and generous woman lying next to me, I foresaw a stable and loving future for us both. We would make up for all that we lacked in our respective pasts because of our complicated families. We would hear and take care of each other. We would create a family of our own.

Suddenly I felt differently about my sexuality. The am-I-this-or-am-I-that question no longer seemed germane. I had loved a number of people up till now, but after a life full of fraught relationships with both men and women, often with impossible and even dangerous complications, I was falling in love with this woman, this Jo Wilder, and this feeling seemed to put an end to all the questions, replacing them with an answer. *Jo and Joel.* I even liked the way our names looked together.

We ended up spending most every night together thereafter, each day falling more in love. It was thrilling and settling to know that there was a real human being with whom I wanted to spend my life and make a family, and after only three weeks of knowing each other, I asked her to marry me. No fanfare. I simply got down on one knee and asked her. And despite the fact that I didn't even have a ring, Jo said yes.

It was an impulsive move. But when I get an idea in my head, nobody can talk me out of it. It's how I've always been. I could have known Jo for days, weeks, or months; it didn't matter. It was about the two of us being right for each other, and of that I had no doubt.

Moving fast also meant I didn't have time to dwell on the previous conflicts I'd had. I believed that whatever attracted me to men would no longer be an issue. That's what I believed, and I was ready to move forward with life.

As soon as Jo said yes I started to plan the wedding. I couldn't wait to be married. I was always *supposed* to be married. It had never been clearer to me, but Jo took a step back almost immediately.

"Why do we have to rush?" she said.

"You're just afraid," I said. "I love you so much. You must know that."

"Why can't we just be engaged?"

"Because I want to marry you and have children with you."

"I can't think about children now. I've got my career."

I thought I had all the answers. The thing I had worked on all those years in therapy was coming true; my history with men had faded into a past narrative. I was finally ready, and the force of my conviction was so strong that no one, not even Jo Wilder, could talk me out of it.

She was scared by the example set by her parents and by her own past difficult relationships with men. But none of those applied to us. We fit like a jigsaw puzzle. Our ages, our interests, our attraction: We were perfect. As for her career, I told her I didn't think that should stop us. No—we could work anything out.

But inside, while I knew Jo was talented, I dreamed about her becoming a wife and mother—not an actress. I convinced myself, from what she had shared with me about how upset the business had made her, that she was too fragile for the theater. I decided that what she needed was someone to take care of her, and if I was anything, I was a caretaker. After dating for less than a month, I couldn't know all her hopes and fears, her inner depth, but I acted "as if." I pushed hard for marriage and convinced her that she'd come to feel it was the right decision.

On the morning of June 29, 1958, Charles McArthur—whom we'd discovered was a mutual friend from class at the Neighborhood Playhouse—and I got up early to head down to Bill's Flower Market, on Sixth Avenue at 28th Street, to pick up armfuls of white margue-rite daisies for our wedding. Jo and I had moved back to New York, which we considered our primary home, since work wasn't happen-ing for either of us in LA.

Charles and his wife Julia, a blonde, were a striking couple from Kansas City. They had generously offered to have the wedding in the living room of their apartment in the fabled Dakota, where they lived with their five children. In my world, the Dakota was a place where anybody would dream of getting married. Steps from Central Park, the extraordinary West Side building was home to many celebrities and architecturally unique.

The McArthurs' apartment was classic old New York. Book-lined and high-ceilinged, with huge windows that offered superb views of the park, the place was grand but not ostentatious. The Browers, how-ever, were not sure about the whole thing. With the shtetl sensibility of those who have never stopped running, they were always beyond sus-picious. Despite the rabbi we hired and the chuppah we had brought into the middle of the living room, the Browers weren't at all sure that this marriage was kosher. Jo's parents, Clara and Izzy, were particu-larly doubtful. Their expectation had always been for their daughter to marry a doctor. Although I was starting to make a name for myself, I was an actor—not at all what they had envisioned for their Joanie. My parents were as thrilled about the marriage as the Browers were upset. Mom and Dad had long ago moved on from the incident with the cantor and any issues it had raised about my sexuality. From there on in, they knew only about the women in my life. Still, they had been concerned in the way that many Jewish parents worry about a grown son who is still single. Now they could relax; both their sons would be married—and to nice, pretty, Jewish girls! Grace and Mickey, instantly embracing Jo, hosted a party in Los Angeles to celebrate our engagement.

Among the thirty-five guests gathered at the Dakota that day was Lotte Lenya, the star of the German stage and screen and Kurt Weill's widow. After her husband's death, in 1950, she had made it her mission to keep his music alive. But it wasn't until Marc Blitzstein's adaptation of *The Threepenny Opera,* four years later, that Lenya became a star in America as well. The show, in which Jo played and became friends with Lenya, ran for nearly seven years.

Amri Galli-Campi, an outrageous former opera singer with whom Jo and I had both taken voice lessons, sang Mozart's "Hallelujah" before the ceremony. But it was Jo who stole the show. It was her moment.

She was a beautiful bride in a white floor-length shirtwaist dress designed for her by Anne Klein, a friend of mine who had given Jo the gown as a wedding gift. I had taken her to the designer's brightly lit showroom, where Anne and I decided what Jo should wear. Jo would have probably picked something much more glamorous than the simple organdy one we settled on, but I had left her no choice.

I began making over Jo's look long before I picked out her wedding dress. It wasn't intentional; I simply couldn't help myself. Almost from the start of our relationship, I didn't think anything of critiquing her clothing. Once when I picked her up for a dinner date, she appeared all done up in a dress, matching bolero jacket, and a matador hat! I thought to myself, *Oh, no, the costumes have got to go.*

"You really can't go out like that," I said.

"What do you mean?"

"The *hat.*"

"I love this hat. Everyone always comments on it."

"I'm sure they do. It's a toreador's hat. Are you going to fight a bull?"

"Well then, go without me."

"I'm sorry. I was just trying to help. Wear whatever you want."

I could see tears edging in from the corners of her eyes.

"Darling, all I mean is that this isn't a fancy event. You know that blue dress you have? You always look stunning in that."

Jo returned to her bedroom, probably relieved to get away from me, and reappeared in a few minutes wearing the blue dress.

"You are so beautiful. I am the luckiest man in the world."

"Thank you," she said in a tone that was, rightly, more confused than happy.

I didn't think about her feelings or the fact that I had shamed her. I was just happy that she wasn't wearing the hat.

Why was I such a bully? I was clearly very concerned that we convey the image of normalcy. That nothing be out of place. All I knew at the time was that when I looked at Jo, I saw only silly shapes and crazy colors marring her beauty. They were piles of unneeded items in an otherwise elegant room, and I set about tidying it up. I was pushy and insensitive as I got rid of her clothes and made her into a classier, simpler, more Mainbocher version of her original image, and I was pleased with myself. When I saw Jo in Anne's dress on the day of our wedding, I cried. She looked so beautiful and, yes, so understated.

The rest of our wedding day and night was pure magic. That evening my dad was a hero, speaking to Jo's grandfather in Yiddish, and giving a dinner for twelve at Danny's Hideaway, the steakhouse of the moment. It was the kind of place where Sammy Davis Jr. and Liberace could be spotted in one corner and Yogi Berra and Mickey Mantle in another. The owner, Dante "Danny" Stradella, had become a friend of mine and sent out Italian specialties cooked by his mama in the kitchen.

After the wedding dinner, Jo and I headed to the Algonquin for our wedding night. The hotel, favored by literary and theatrical circles, was perfect for a pair of New York newlyweds like us. What could be more glamorous than the place where Dorothy Parker and the rest of the writers, actors, and critics who made up the Algonquin Round Table met daily for great conversation and unparalleled wit? Because I had often stayed at the hotel before I had my own apartment in New York, the owners, the Bodnes, gave us the bridal suite as a wedding present. Everything was in place: the City, the wedding, the suite, the wife.

The start of our marriage was as fun and unique as our wedding. Our first apartment was a studio on the second floor of a walkup at 8 Jones Street in Greenwich Village. Although small, it had a fireplace and just enough room for Jo, me, and her Yorkie, Pablo. We immediately drove out to Bucks County, Pennsylvania, to look for a big antique brass bed. Successful in our mission, we found a beautiful bed that was so tarnished it was nearly black. (We applied Noxon Metal Polish to it once we got it home—then we spent a week trying to get the fumes out of the tiny apartment.) We felt slightly Bohemian in the Village, which was having its moment at the time.

The people on the streets didn't look at all like the people uptown. Especially in the summer, it was like one large party with everyone out on their stoops, playing music, smoking, hanging out. Jo and I loved to walk around Washington Square Park on romantic, warm nights, soaking up the beautiful scene of young women in peasant tops, men in beards, and guitars playing folk music that floated through the evening.

Despite the social and political upheaval of the time and place, Jo and I lived a pretty domestic existence. We both loved to cook and had friends, usually couples, over often. I was certainly Grace's son when it came to food. Shopping along West 4th Street and Bleecker, we found all the great bakeries, butchers, and vegetable and fruit markets, which were like the one Grandpa Epstein had run in Cleveland. Food was only one area of exploration in our pursuit of good things. We dove into art, ballet, opera, design—all those things that are so special, adventurous, and available in New York.

Once the initial excitement of our newly married life was over, Jo and I still had our sources of conflict. As with most other couples, our problems were there from the beginning of our relationship. In particular, we continued to argue over Jo's ambitions as an actress and her fear that having a family would hold her back from pursuing her career. She experienced the vacillations normal for any actor. And as she went from the high of playing the title role in *Peter Pan,* to much success in summer stock, to the very deep low of being turned down for yet another Broadway role, I played up her uncertainty about whether she had the grit and determination to make it in the theater. I never married Jo for her to be a star; I was clear from the onset that I wanted her to devote herself to being a wife and mother. I thought I was being practical, that this path was best for our family. It is hard enough, I reasoned, for one person in a couple to be in the theater, a profession that is so uncertain, stressful, and consuming.

When Jo did work, I was anything but supportive. When she was in a Midwestern summer stock production of *Flower Drum Song,* I flew out to visit her—and took along my laundry! I'm ashamed about it now, but back then I didn't think twice about carrying my dirty clothes onto the plane for her to wash. Again, I thought I was simply being practical; I didn't have time to do it before the trip, and I knew there was a washing machine in every theater. But arriving with my full laundry bag was a clear message to Jo, who was rightly stunned and furious.

"I can't believe you!" she said. "Bringing your laundry to where I'm working? Are you crazy?"

"I had no time to do it."

"So you brought it for *me* to do?"

"No, I am going to do it," I said. "Just show me where the washing machine is."

And that was it. In our fights, there was always so much we left unsaid. Both of us did anything we could to avoid an explosion. We dealt with each other by *not* saying how we really felt, *not* saying the worst. The worst, for me, was that I didn't want to go to the Midwest to visit her in summer stock. I didn't like being the husband of the actress. I didn't want her to be working. Although we never discussed it outright, it was clear she understood that with my dirty laundry, I was saying, "You know where you belong and it's not here."

Again I was acting like a bully, but in the end I got what I wanted. Within our first year of marriage, Jo got pregnant, and nothing could have made me happier. I had wanted her to get pregnant on our wedding night—I whispered to her, "I hope we made a baby tonight." We wound up conceiving during the run of a production of *Tom Sawyer* in Sacramento's Music Circus in which I played Huckleberry Finn and she was Becky Thatcher, Tom's girlfriend. The situation was so ludicrous that both of us had a lot of trouble keeping a straight face for the entire run. We were still in the first flush of marriage, and everything made us laugh. It wasn't our finest work, but we weren't doing Ibsen, for God's sake.

Jo's growing belly was not only the promise of fatherhood but also further proof that I could finally put behind me all the complexities of my childhood and the fear and self-doubt I'd felt for so long. But the pregnancy wasn't easy. From the beginning, Jo experienced complications, and the doctor ordered immediate bed rest. By this point, we had moved uptown, to 865 First Avenue, at 49th Street, a step we hoped toward a more sophisticated New York life. My great friend Larry Kert, who had originated the role of Tony in *West Side Story*, tipped us off about an apartment available in his building.

I'd met Larry when we were just teenagers trying to make it in LA. Though I could have been the Juvenile Star of *Borscht Capades*, he was singing with Bill Norvis and the Upstarts. From the start, Larry was the funniest, loosest, most handsome and talented person I'd ever known. Everybody was drawn to him. A good horseback rider and excellent gymnast, he was thoroughly masculine. And he was gay, openly gay, even in his teens. He was one of the few young guys I'd met who was so comfortable with himself that his sexuality didn't seem to be a problem for him.

To me, that was nothing short of a miracle. I was envious of how he embraced his homosexuality, but his experience had no bearing on mine. His family was 100 percent supportive of him. They knew who he was and loved him anyway. That was beyond my comprehension. While I envied his openness, I felt as if the same behavior would never have been accepted from me.

What Larry and I did share was a desire to be on Broadway, where we both struggled to get jobs in the theater. Although we didn't talk all the time, we checked in with each other periodically, and whenever we did, it was affectionate. Larry and I adored each other.

Years before I met Jo, when I had first moved to New York and was looking for work, Larry and I went out for dinner one night, and we talked for so long that it got too late for him to go home. We wound up back at the Belvedere Hotel, where I was living, and we slept together. It was sexy and brotherly at once. The radio was playing "Danny Boy," and when I woke in the morning he was gone, but I found a note by my toothbrush, signed "Danny Boy." Sleeping together didn't change our relationship; it just made it better. We never stopped caring about each other. When Larry landed the historic role of Tony in *West Side Story*, I went to a run-through of the brilliant musical in New York, without sets and costumes, and then to the out-of-town opening in Washington before its Broadway debut, in 1955.

Larry was living with a dancer, Grover Dale, by the time Jo and I moved to First Avenue. He was part of his own world, where he could be openly gay in his private life. (Everyone supported him. His sister Anita Ellis, a renowned jazz singer, and her husband, Mort, were so close to Larry that they lived in the building, too.) And I was part of my world. The situation between us was never tense. Whenever I was around Larry, I didn't feel that he felt sorry for me or believed that I was living a lie. Just like any other friend, Larry was happy that I seemed to be getting what I wanted and needed from my marriage. And Jo loved him, too. Everybody did.

Jo and I began fixing up our new flat. She had bought a big drawing by Rico Lebrun before we met that I loved, too (she always had a great eye for art). The burlap wallpaper we put up made all our art look great. It was also a great canvas for the furniture we purchased from Design Research, a Boston shop at the forefront of Scandinavian design, where we picked up a modern teak sideboard. We squirreled away money for the finer things, such as our first-anniversary lunch, at Lutèce. Although the French restaurant, famous for its haute cuisine, was only down the street from our apartment, it made us feel as if we were in Paris for the afternoon.

No matter how tastefully our apartment was designed, Jo was miserable while confined to it during the difficult pregnancy. When I returned home after an entire day out—auditioning for an Off Broadway play; lunching with Charlie Baker at the Oak Room, around the corner from William Morris; and working on some new material with a writer for the act—I found Jo lying on the bed per doctor's orders. She was at her wit's end. "I told you," she said. "I knew we should never have done this. You were rushing."

I felt horrible. Jo was imprisoned in a world of discomfort into which I had forced her. Through the anger and accusations, I could see that she was really frightened. We both were. She didn't respond to my attempts to make her feel better with tenderness and humor, and I couldn't blame her. This had all been my idea, not hers. It was my fault, because she hadn't wanted to be pregnant, just as she hadn't wanted to get married. The guilt of seeing my wife lying in bed day after day was bad, but nothing compared with what lay ahead.

She was in her sixth month when in the middle of the night she woke up in pain. Weeping, she was having contractions. At 3:00 A.M. we rushed to the New York Medical College hospital, where we were met by our obstetrician, Dr. Vincent Merendino.

Jo endured a nightmarish labor. And as I watched my wife writhing in pain, Vinnie explained that he didn't want to give her too much anesthetic, because of the added risk to the baby, who was already in peril. I thought about The Sisters, my mother, and the voice planted inside my head long ago saying somehow it was always my fault. I was heartbroken watching Jo in so much misery, particularly because she was not a complainer. She never wanted to be that vulnerable.

After five hours, she gave birth to a one-and-a-half-pound boy, whom we named Jeremy.

When Jo, worn out from the punishing labor, had finally fallen asleep, I went to the neonatal intensive-care unit to see our baby lying in an incubator. It was like looking at something out of a science-fiction film. I sat staring at him, this incredibly tiny human being, thinking, *How could this be?* Everything from Jeremy's traumatic entrance into this world to the size of his feet was unbelievable. I left his side only to return to Jo.

Two days after our son's birth, I was scheduled to open at the Diplomat Hotel, in Hollywood, Florida. I was about to call William Morris to cancel when Vinnie advised otherwise. According to the neonatal experts at the hospital, there was nothing inherently wrong with Jeremy other than his weight. In any case, he would need to be in an incubator for weeks.

"It is just a matter of time," Vinnie said to me as we talked in a corner of the hospital room where Jo was turning down the tray being brought to her by a nurse. "Each day is one more day that he is closer to being out of danger. But this is going to be very challenging, and there is actually very little you can do here." He also thought it would be best for Jo and me to be together and for her to accompany me to Florida. I was left to make all the decisions, since Jo couldn't even eat, let alone think; she was so exhausted and sad. It was impossible in that moment to make the right decision. I had no idea what that even was. It seemed crazy for me to keep the job and take Jo in her fragile state on an airplane. But her OB had suggested I do just that, and in times of great trauma and confusion, it's normal to default to a passive position and follow doctor's orders. So I heeded Dr. Merendino's advice to go to work and take my wife. We flew to Florida the next day.

After we arrived at the Diplomat, I made sure Jo, still in a lot of pain, was comfortable before I went down to the showroom to do a sound check. My performance that night was like nothing I had ever experienced. All the words, music, and jokes were there, but I wasn't. I was on automatic pilot, the body doing its job and the mind somewhere else.

After the first show, I ran back up to the room to check on Jo, who was still in a lot of discomfort. I saw that she had had a little water and melon. We didn't talk much but that was all right. What was there to say? It was too horrible to talk.

When I returned to the room after the second show, completely depleted, the lights were low. I turned them out, and after a few minutes lying quietly together in the dark, she said in a still, small voice, "Dr. Merendino's office called."

"What's wrong?"

"He said they did everything they could."

"What? What do you mean?"

"The baby is dead."

And that was it. That was all we said. Those two nightmarish words hanging above us in the dark took up all the space.

As irrational as it was, I never imagined that we would lose our child. Even when he appeared so impossibly small. Even when he was in an incubator. "Each day," the experts said, "was a success." And that's all I heard. I had wanted that baby so much, since I held that little girl at the Sovereign Hotel.

If I had allowed myself to know how I felt, I never would have left Jeremy's side or dragged Jo to Florida for a nightclub act. In that dark hotel room filled with grief, Jo and I held each other and wept.

In my arms, her whole body shivered, her injury complete. I had promised to take care of her, to make her happy, to let nothing bad befall her. And here, feeling this little shaking thing pressed up against me, I realized that I had done just the opposite. I would have done anything in that moment to change what had happened, even though I knew that there was in fact nothing, just nothing, I could do.

I was helpless and culpable, a father and not a father. When a terrible thing you can't imagine—such as the death of a child—actually happens, it becomes a part of you forever. Jeremy's death didn't just shatter my confidence but my very core. The belief I had always had in myself—pushing to find a place for myself in the theater, where I wasn't sure I was wanted; exploring my sexual desire for men but pushing past it to find the woman of my dreams; persuading Jo to follow me into this adventure of marriage and family—was gone. It was gone, all of it, because I had failed Jo and my son.

I wept with joy and disbelief that our little girl—Jennifer—was in my arms. *Now we will be happy,* I thought. *Everything is just right.*

CHAPTER EIGHT

At 3:00 A.M. the phone next to the bed in our apartment on First Avenue started ringing. I had come in from LA for three days in late March of 1960 to play a date in the Catskills (always a dependable source of some quick cash) and gone to sleep early, knowing that the show tomorrow at Brown's Hotel in Loch Sheldrake would go late. Irritated, I picked up the receiver, hearing from afar the operator saying something about a collect call, before I hung it back up.

A few seconds later, it was ringing again. A little more awake this time, I heard Maury Lazarus, our friend and new obstetrician, his voice a tad testy, saying to the operator, "Tell him his wife just had a baby and that he should accept the call."

That couldn't be. When I had left Jo, in high spirits, less than twenty-four hours earlier, our baby hadn't been due for another six weeks. I couldn't bear the idea of missing the birth, and, even worse, the possibility that again something had gone wrong.

We had lost our infant son a little more than a year earlier, and Jo and I didn't speak about it often. We were both too sad. A few months after it happened, I had to travel to England, and when I was there I decided she needed a distraction—in the form of a puppy. I know it was silly, but we needed cheering up. I had planned to surprise Jo with it upon my return. I had heard that the best Yorkshire terriers were bred by a Mrs. Ethel Mundy, and an English pal drove me way out into the country to her house in Wallington Surrey. When I rang the bell, twenty tiny Yorkies went berserk, yapping until Mrs. Mundy commanded, "That'll be sufficient." Immediate silence followed—it was very funny. I left with a three-month-old I named Alfie. (The night before I had seen the brilliant actor Alfie Lynch perform in *Oh, What a Lovely War!* at the Theater Royal Stratford East.)

Other than Alfie and our other Yorkie, Pablo, there was little that Jo and I found to love after we lost our son. We were shattered, and because the hole was so large that nothing could fill it, we sadly took it out on each other. So the grief, which had momentarily connected us in that Florida hotel room, began to tear us apart.

There were many silent fights and petty squabbles. We couldn't agree on the simplest things, such as where to go to dinner or if we should go visit friends in the country for the weekend. In every decision or discussion I was looking for signs of accusation on her part. I spent so much time blaming myself, and taking full responsibility for everything that happened, that my guilt informed every aspect of our lives. I walked on eggshells, worried about setting her off. The result was that she reverted to the life she led before we were married. She resumed her singing lessons, went to yoga more often, and started calling her agent for auditions. We didn't see each other much during the day, and when we came together at night it was often with friends who acted as a buffer.

It was amazing, therefore, that we decided to try for another baby. Like so many other couples, we never discussed getting pregnant again but instead relied on the nonverbal cues husband and wife give each other when they are too afraid to have direct communication. Maybe both of us knew on some level that if we were going to stay together that we would have to replace that loss. It would have been easy to simply drift further and further apart. So as time passed and the pain subsided, Jo and I found room to give each other another chance.

Within the year Jo got pregnant again, and we became obsessed with learning everything there was to know about natural childbirth. That we allowed ourselves to love each other again felt like a real gift, and I wanted to do everything I could to honor that. At Lamaze class, we got to know the other couples. With the realization that their hopes and dreams were so much like ours, we started to feel wonderfully ordinary. As Jo practiced getting into different birthing positions and I tried out massage techniques, we were like any other expectant parents. While we could never forget about Jeremy, we weren't a couple grieving but one with a child on the way. I came to love those classes full of heavy breathing, learning how I could help Jo. I was no longer powerless.

After Maury woke me up in the middle of the night to relay the news that Jo had given birth to a healthy baby girl, I immediately called and woke up the Catskills impresario and agent Charlie Rapp, because I was getting on the first flight to LA. I had missed the main event, but I couldn't miss another second. I had a daughter!

When I arrived at the hospital, Jo was just waking up. Radiant and happy, she held the most perfectly formed child with little bee-stung lips. I wept with joy and disbelief that our little girl—Jennifer—was in my arms. *Now we will be happy,* I thought. *Everything is just right.*

Jennifer was a very good baby, and I took her everywhere with me, to the dry cleaner, lunch, the park to walk the dogs, wherever I went—always stating proudly to anyone who would listen, "This is my daughter." I was enthralled by every aspect of caring for her, from diapering to bathing to giving her a bottle in the middle of the night. I was finally getting to do all those things that I had been good at as an eight-year-old at the Sovereign. Nothing ever made me so happy and whole. Settling into family life, I was in total heaven—complete. Even if Jo was cranky, I had Jennifer.

Our arguments continued to center on the question of Jo's working. Whenever she got a call about an audition, there was a moment of whether she should or shouldn't go.

"You don't want me to, do you?" she asked, as if she believed that by asking me the same question again and again, she might get a different answer.

"You know how I feel," I said. "But you do what you have to do."

Jo would always make up her own mind about whether or not to go on an audition. If she didn't go, she would be angry that she might have missed an opportunity. But if she went and didn't get the part, she would be depressed. Either way, there was great upset at home.

I was getting a lot of work in television. Because of that, we returned to living full time in Los Angeles, where, not long after Jennifer's birth, a wonderful little house we heard about was going on the market. Having a new baby, we wanted to settle into a home, so we bought the Mexican hacienda on an acre up on Woodrow Wilson Drive with a big assist from Jo's father, Izzy. The plain stucco house was very small, but its windows looked out on a hill full of flowers, Italian cypress trees, and bright bursts of bougainvillea.

My parents came over a couple of times a week to fuss over the baby. Although my mother was a steamroller, Jo got along well with her. Grace loved to bring Jennifer little gifts such as a silver rattle or a china cup that she had painted herself. I was able to put the past I had with my mother aside enough that I truly enjoyed their visits. It made me happy to see my parents with my daughter in the picture of normalcy that I had always wanted.

I was more motivated than ever to make a living, which I did in a string of parts on Westerns, such as *Bronco,* and *Lawman.* All my guest roles were on Warner Bros. TV shows, where I got my start in 1959 when I was cast in *Maverick,* the comedy Western series about Texas poker players, which was in the top ten at the time. I got the part of Billy the Kid, which was, to say the least, creative casting. Although my father was a cowboy in *Borscht Capades,* I was not your typical outlaw.

I was thrilled about the role, so I never mentioned that I'd never ridden a horse before—and God, was I scared of horses! Particularly the gigantic, bucking ones they had on set. I hadn't told the producers or director I didn't know how to ride for fear they'd get someone to replace me. Thinking fast, I suggested that it might be interesting if I rode on the back of another rider's horse. Well, the director loved the idea. But it didn't turn out exactly as I had imagined. In the scene where we, the bad guys, make a getaway, a stuntman rode the horse fast, took hold of me, and pulled me up behind him. It was so much worse than if I had just got on the damn horse myself! Thank God they got the shot on the first take.

The best part of working on *Maverick*, other than the subsequent roles it prompted, was becoming friends with James Garner. To the outside world we couldn't have been more different. For starters, Jim was six feet two and I am five five. We made an odd couple wherever we went. Once, at a party, he and I went into a bedroom, traded clothes, and came out—ta da! Everyone laughed at my pants, which looked like shorts on Jim. We were like brothers with a slightly sick sense of humor.

In Jim, I found not only an unassuming charmer but also a fellow hardworking husband with small children, pursuing a tough career in the toughest place, Hollywood. Jo got on with Jim's wife, Lois, and our families became close.

I loved our life on Woodrow Wilson Drive, working, making dinner with friends, waking up at dawn with our daughter. So it was with much difficulty that in the summer of 1960, when Jennifer was six months old, I left for Italy to film *Come September*. The movie boasted glamorous locations of Rome and Santa Margherita Ligure on the Italian Riviera, and a cast that starred Rock Hudson as a wealthy American businessman who spends each September with his Italian mistress, Gina Lollobrigida, at his villa by the sea. I had a role as a smart-aleck college kid (I was still playing a teenager even though I was twenty-eight!) who is part of a group of American students staying at the villa.

The part wasn't much, but I took the job because I wanted to work with the director, Robert Mulligan, who was just off an artistic success with *Fear Strikes Out*, starring Anthony Perkins. Over the years, I've made a lot of movies for very little money and not much in the script for me, either, hoping that despite the size of the part and the pay just above scale, I could make an impact as I had with *About Face*. I already had a reputation as someone who didn't just say my lines and call it a day. My input could be annoying, but it also could end up adding something valuable.

At the time of *Come September* I wanted more film work. The TV work had been paying the bills, but it was still only small parts. I had to continue to find a way to succeed and vowed to myself to make an impact on this movie. So when Bob shot a scene of the college kids, myself included, zipping through the hills of Santa Margherita Ligure on a Vespa, I gave it the old *as if.* I was less than comfortable on the motorized scooter, with a girl behind me holding on to my waist, but I didn't dare tell anyone. It was not unlike getting on that horse in *Maverick*. And I wasn't thrilled in another scene that had us wading into the Tiber's freezing water, where raw sewage floated freely. But I wasn't going to complain!

Working with Rock Hudson made up for swimming in the polluted river. After years of playing heroes and heartthrobs, he proved he was also a comedian when he starred in *Pillow Talk*—from the same writers who did *Come September*—which had come out the year before. Although he kept mostly to himself while in Italy, we ran lines on occasion and once went out to dinner at a nondescript trattoria. Again, there was that thing between us, that sixth, seventh, or eighth sense. It was never discussed, but we had a secret, built-in camaraderie, which combined intimacy and anonymity, as if you were telling your deepest secrets to the person sitting next to you on Flight 001 from New York to LA. He was full of seemingly contradictory qualities. Open and friendly and yet at the same time closeted and careful, he loved to laugh: big (like him), boisterous guffaws. But as soon as the camera was ready, Rock, the consummate professional, was, too.

Come September wound up doing well at the box office. The real-life romance between the movie's young stars, Bobby Darin and Sandra Dee, was a publicist's dream. The hipster singer-songwriter fell head over heels for the *Gidget* star on the set of his first film, and in the stuff from which Hollywood legends are made, they married three months later. The movie might have been a professional success for me, but it sent my personal life into disarray.

While I was shooting *Come September* in Italy, Jo got a job in a San Francisco production of *Threepenny Opera*. Work was always nosing its way back into her life with calls for auditions. But she didn't have to audition for this part; she was asked to re-create a role with which she had great success when the show played Off-Broadway. There was no discussion about whether or not she would take the job. This was a part she knew. She was thrilled and said yes immediately.

For the nearly two months that she was up north with our six-month-old daughter and I was in Italy, we were uncomfortably out of touch, communicating but not really. Calling overseas wasn't simple with the time change, but when we did talk, there was too much air on the phone. The old conflicts returned. I didn't want her to work, let alone take our new baby on the road. Miserable and missing my daughter, I became paranoid. Who would be watching my child? The distance compounded my worries.

When we returned home from our different worlds, we were like strangers. Before we were married, Jo once mused that I might turn into her very own Richard Halliday. Halliday, who gave up his career as a studio executive to manage the career of his wife, the Broadway star Mary Martin, was her dream husband. Forget that Halliday was well known to be homosexual or that I didn't want to do anything of the sort. I vetoed the plan immediately. "Those are two very different people from us," I said.

"I know that," Jo said.

When she started working again, I wondered if she still harbored the fantasy that, like Halliday, I valued her talent as an artist above all else. Although she was a wonderful actress and singer, to me she was first and foremost a wife and mother. I don't know what kept me from seeing that she could have been all four. Was I trying to keep safe from a too-powerful woman, an issue that started with my mother?

The conflict between Jo and me over her career reached a crossroads at about the time I got my first opportunity to be on Broadway. It all began when I received a call in the winter of 1961 from Charlie Baker, who told me to come east to audition for the replacement of one of the leads in Neil Simon's first Broadway smash, *Come Blow Your Horn*.

Although we still had the house on Woodrow Wilson, Jo, Jennifer, and I returned to New York for this opportunity. The cast was filled with New York theater veterans such as Lou Jacobi (who played the father) and Pert Kelton (the mother). The up-and-coming young actor Ron Rifkin was my understudy (and became a lifelong friend). I never heard such laughter from an audience in my life. I played hundreds of performances, and each night the laughter was so intense I felt my eyeballs vibrate.

Not long after the play ended, I went to London where I saw Anthony Newley play the circus clown Littlechap in *Stop the World—I Want to Get Off*. I loved everything about the musical—the score, the pantomime, the character, and Newley. He and Leslie Bricusse had written the book, music, and lyrics. In the first act, Littlechap is a charmer, but through his cheating ways, he loses his wife and later his world. He sits alone at the end of the show in a single spot near the edge of the stage and sings "What Kind of Fool Am I." It's a show-stopper and in the last minutes, all is forgiven by the audience.

Littlechap was one of those dark, deeply flawed characters, such as King Lear or Willy Loman, who are always magnets for actors. So when I learned that Newley wasn't going on the national tour, I auditioned (in full makeup) and got the part, and I knew immediately it could be a career changer.

It was hard for me to play Littlechap exactly as Newley had. His version—in which he borrowed heavily from Marcel Marceau, the mime of the moment—was highly stylized. I, on the other hand, was essentially a New York-trained actor. My way of finding a character was to create a biography and have compassion for his flawed nature. It was easy with Littlechap. A clown, trying to be a success, wanting children, cheating on his wife, and feeling devastated after her death because he truly loved her? My identification was strong and immediate. During "What Kind of Fool Am I?," one of the great ballads of musical theater, I regretted his mistakes and losses as if they were my own.

Over the eight months of the 1963 national tour of *Stop the World*, I found my own Littlechap, and it struck a chord with audiences and the press. "How is it that you always end up all alone on the stage in a spotlight?" asked an amazed Hal Prince, the renowned theater producer and director, who had come to see the play later that year in Westport.

My parents came to see me when I played *Stop the World* in LA. *Borscht Capades* was no longer running, but Dad put together a huge holiday show every year, *Chanukah in Santa Monica*, which was held at the Santa Monica Civic Auditorium. Still, Mother was always looking out for his image. When they came to see me backstage after the performance, she ordered my father to "stand up straight, Mickey!" When Dad drew me in for a hug, I could also see that she had put very subtle pancake on him. That was something she did when she felt he looked too pale—that and insist he wear a hairpiece onstage.

Besides a chance to be with the folks, Los Angeles was a very important stop on the tour. The good reviews I got from the LA critics turned out to have some gravitas with the New York theater community. For the first time since *On Borrowed Time*, I was being taken seriously as an actor. I should have been happy, but I was far from it.

When I was touring with *Stop the World*, Jo auditioned for the Broadway musical *She Loves Me*, directed by Hal Prince. She was hired to be Barbara Cook's understudy and given a small part of her own. So she stayed in New York with Jennifer, and again, we found ourselves working in separate cities, which I believed threatened our marriage. Families didn't live separate lives, and I couldn't stop worrying about us. My mind went crazy with thoughts of her having affairs—I knew what happened in the theater, that very sexy place. She would fall in love with someone else, leave me, and take Jennifer. I'd be left with nothing. I tried to talk myself out of how I felt, which I knew to be irrational and without basis. But my only life was the stage between 8:00 P.M. and 11:00 P.M. With the rest of my day empty, I filled it by worrying. The loneliness of the road reinforced my emotional state until it verged on depression.

When the tour stopped in Chicago for an eight-week engagement, I was near some sort of breakdown. In the days leading up to the opening night I grew emotionally frail. I withdrew from the life of the show, retreating from the cast even though I felt responsible to them. Weepy most of the time, I lost my appetite. I had daily sessions over the phone with the therapist I had been seeing for the past four years. Although I told myself that I had resolved the issue of my sexual identity, I continued to go to therapy to deal with challenges in my marriage as well as my career. Just like my father, I was always worried about work. Now, for the first time, I had a part that showed all the different sides of me as an actor, one that could bring me the recognition I had sought for so long, and I was destroying it with doubts about my personal life.

I panicked that I wouldn't be able to perform. The thought that I might not be able to fulfill my obligation to the cast, producers, and audience kept me up at night. Littlechap rarely left the stage. Letting everyone down now would surely ruin my future. A perfect situation for the onset of stage fright.

When I called Jo the day before opening night in Chicago, I was having a full-blown panic attack and needed her right away. "I know I can't go on if you don't come," I said. "I can't do it. Whatever it is, neurotic or crazy. The truth is I'm lost without you and Jen." In hindsight it was beyond manipulative essentially to force Jo to choose between keeping her job and keeping me from a breakdown. But in that moment, I really felt as if I was dying.

What could Jo do? She was on the first plane she could get. I was a blubbering, pathetic mess when she arrived. We talked way into the night, trying not to wake Jennifer, who was sleeping in the other room. Taking my hand, Jo said, "I can't bear to see you like this."

She didn't make any big declarations about the future but said she would quit the show and stay with me. That was enough for me. I had spent so much time and energy carefully constructing a narrative of the perfect family—beginning way before I had even met Jo, during those early therapy sessions in Gertrude's garden office. Anything that countered that narrative threatened my existence.

Jo made a big sacrifice to reunite our family and let me finally establish myself as an actor in the theater. Even though I hadn't yet originated a role on Broadway, my performance of Littlechap on the road was a great success. I vowed to use the opportunity my wife had given me to do good things and make her proud.

Meanwhile, Jo decided she wanted another child, but it was too risky for her to go through another pregnancy because of the previous complications. Undeterred, she began exploring adoption, a gutsy act that wasn't very common back then. As she did all the research, locating agencies and a lawyer, she became convinced of the urgency of transforming the life of a child born under sad and dark circumstances. I was conflicted. I was unfortunately swayed by the old prejudices and fears of the problems that can come when claiming a stranger's child as one's own. Yet adopting a child would give Jo a purpose other than acting.

Then in September of 1964, the adoption lawyer called out of the blue with the news that a baby boy was about to be born in LA to a sixteen-year-old girl who was all alone in the world. When the infant arrived, I was afraid to go to the hospital. I didn't think I could go through with this. But as soon as the nurse in the maternity ward pointed through the glass to this helpless little baby, I nearly collapsed with emotion and then immediately went into rescue mode. "Let's take him and go," I said to Jo. We named our new son James Rico—his middle name in honor of the artist Rico Lebrun, who made the large drawing she had bought years ago.

James was a beautiful addition to our wonderful family. But the bigger and better parts that I thought were going to follow my success in *Stop the World* never came. It wasn't that the offers I received weren't good enough; I didn't receive *any* offers at all. Zero. Zip. It was confusing. There had been real motion to my run as Littlechap, fueled by a lot of heavy-duty acknowledgment from the theater community. But instead of being seen as a Broadway commodity, it was as if I had become invisible. And it wasn't just in the theater but also in movies and TV. There was *nothing* on the horizon.

I had always had financial ups and downs throughout my career. That is generally the actor's lot. Very rarely does something happen (such as a hit television series that runs for years, tantamount to an annuity) that keeps a performer from ever having to worry again. That was certainly never my experience, and at this point, while faced with a new baby, a four-year-old daughter starting nursery school, and absolutely no prospects, I found the economics of art troubling.

It wasn't until the summer of 1966 that I finally got a job. It was a God-awful job, but I had to take it; we needed the money. I played a pirate—a comedy pirate—in an outdoor spectacle posing as a musical. *Mardi Gras* played seven long nights a week (rain or shine) at the Jones Beach Marine Theatre, outdoors on Long Island, where a small body of water separated the stage from the audience.

To call this mess a musical would be an insult to the art form. The jokes were bad; the lyrics were banal; the music was derivative. Louis Armstrong was the draw. That meant that at some time during Act 2, he was brought on to sing three or four crowd-pleasers that had nothing to do with the story, which was not very complicated to begin with.

Every day at three in the afternoon I boarded a bus that went out to Jones Beach as if I were on my way to work in the coal mines, depressed by the knowledge that I would not be on the return bus until two in the morning. Sitting in the inevitable and excruciating traffic on the Long Island Expressway, I tried to figure out just how I had ended up here.

I wanted to be in the theater to shock, expand, make life more interesting. With Wynn Handman, a former Neighborhood Playhouse member who carried on the teachings of Sanford Meisner, I performed in one of the first experimental plays of his new theater. In *Harry, Noon and Night*, a wild and woolly play written by Ronald Ribman, I played an American soldier in Berlin opposite Dustin Hoffman, making his debut, as a transsexual German. As an actor I love to surprise, and the audience was surprised—to say the least—when I tied Dustin up in a blanket and sat on him.

And now I was doing a poorly executed, badly staged soft-shoe as a hokey pirate in a show where most had paid the price of admission only to hear the great Satchmo sing "What a Wonderful World." Was I just not good enough to do anything better?

On the bus ride home along the choked expressway, while the rest of the cast slept, I started to rethink all of it. Maybe the theater wasn't my destiny after all. I had a wife and small children who deserved more than a comedy pirate as a husband and father. Tomorrow I would lay out all the possibilities—an art gallery owner, an agent, a hand model, a tummler in the Catskills. Anything other than this.

"There's a part I think you'll be just swell for."

CHAPTER NINE

Even though it was two in the afternoon, I was asleep when the phone rang. Depressed, I considered not answering. A few days earlier, *Mardi Gras* had closed, and though I was grateful not to be battling traffic on the LIE or playing a crappy pirate, at least it was a paycheck. Now, facing financial as well as artistic trouble, I was plunged into a state of despair.

"Hello," I said.

"Joely!"

"Hal?"

Hal Prince was the only person in the world other than my aunt Jean who called me by that name.

"What's wrong?" the theater director asked. "You don't sound like yourself."

"I'm all right, just a little under . . . You know, same old, same old . . . Work."

"Well that's good. Then I get to be the bearer of good news. This is perfect timing, pal! Remember last week at Downey's, I told you I'm working on a new show?"

"*I Am a Camera*. I saw Julie Harris in it, in '51."

"Exactly! Well it's happening!"

Hal—who had already established himself as one of the top musical-theater producers, changing the shape of the genre with the likes of *Fiddler on the Roof* and *West Side Story*—went on to say that my old friends Fred Ebb and John Kander had written a brilliant score. Joe Masteroff, who had won a Tony nomination for his musical comedy *She Loves Me*, had written the book. The young choreographer Ron Field was set to stage the musical numbers.

"And there's a role we think you'd be swell for!"

His words just kind of hung there.

"So cheer up, pal! We're all going to hear the score at John's in a few days. Annette in the office will call you, and I'll see you there! Judy sends love, and—oh, yes! We're calling it *Cabaret*." And with that, he hung up.

That was a Tuesday. On Thursday, I found myself in a cab going to John Kander's townhouse in the West 70s to hear the score. Equal parts nervous and excited, I had the hiccups, which I never got. This might actually lead to something—not just something, *the* thing I had been dreaming about for so long.

I had previously enjoyed seeing John and Fred demonstrate their material. Together, the brilliant duo (who knew each other so well that they practically finished each other's sentences) could sing and sell you the Brooklyn Bridge. I had known both men long before they became well known. Before Broadway, Fred was *the* go-to guy for special material for nightclub acts. When he helped me with mine, Fred was appealing and truly funny. John and I became friendly while he was still writing dance arrangements. From back home in Kansas City, he knew Charles McArthur (who, with his wife, Julia, had so generously welcomed a chuppah in their apartment at the Dakota), and John had been kind enough to accompany me in the pit for some of my many failed Broadway auditions.

When I arrived at John's handsome duplex, he opened the door, and we hugged. The room, packed with people involved in the show, had a

New Year's Eve vibe, with everyone hugging and kissing and anticipating. Hal walked over to the piano, shushed the crowd, gave a few words of welcome, and offered a brief synopsis of *Cabaret*: Like the play, *I Am a Camera*, the musical was based on Christopher Isherwood's *The Berlin Stories*, an autobiographical novel set in 1930s Berlin as it teetered on the precipice of one of the worst moments in history. Then Hal introduced "the boys," Freddie and John. Some people found seats, others stood, but all were at attention. John sat at the piano and arranged his music while faithful Fred watched him with obvious respect and affection.

Dead quiet.

John played a low tremolo on the piano, like that of a drumroll slowly growing louder and lower, which ended in a mimicked cymbal crash of the higher keys on the register. Then he began the vamp.

Oom-pah-pah, oom-pah-pah
Oom-pah-pah, oom-pah-pah
Oom-pah-pah, oom-pah-pah
Oom-pah-pah, oom-pah-pah

Fred turned to us and sang:
"Willkommen! Bienvenue, welcome! Fremder, etranger, stranger . . ."
Even from the vamp—the song didn't sound like anything anyone had ever heard before. There was pandemonium before John and Fred had a chance to finish "Willkommen." Meanwhile I was thinking, *That song is going to be mine.* We finally quieted down so that they could play the entire score but the room never stopped vibrating.

Hal hadn't said much about my part—the Emcee, as he was called—but I couldn't get over it. This was the first time I'd ever been offered a part in the theater without an audition. So when Hal's office messengered the script to our new apartment, in a townhouse on 30th Street just off Park Avenue (not the fancy part), I opened the envelope immediately. I often procrastinate looking at scripts, but I had already spent so much time imagining this one that I had to read it right away.

With Jo in the kitchen and the kids out in the park with Nellie, our magnificent babysitter, I closed the door to the living room, sat down by one of the tall front windows, and began reading. Sally Bowles, an aspiring actress from England, was the central character. It was her story. That was no surprise. I liked her madcap character as I turned the pages. Her lover, Clifford Bradshaw, had been gay in Isherwood's *Berlin Stories*. But this was 1966, and a gay character on Broadway was not possible. So he was to be a heterosexual American charmer. A few other characters, such as Sally's landlady, Fräulein Schneider, and her Jewish suitor, Herr Schultz, made an appearance in the script, but by the time I arrived at the last pages of Act 1, there was still no indication of the Emcee. I quickly thumbed back through all of Act 1 to see if I had missed something. I hadn't.

I got up and went to the kitchen; I had to get a drink of water before I began Act 2. Back reading, I came to scene 3, a big set change for a glorious follies-like number with five songs—"Willkommen," "Two Ladies," "The Money Song," "Tiller Girls," and "If You Could See Her." All of those great songs I had heard at John's house, which had made a kaleidoscopic impression of nightlife in Berlin during 1929, were the sum total of the Emcee's part. My character had no interaction with Sally, Cliff, Schneider, Schultz, or anyone else in the play other than the Kit Kat Klub dancers and band. No words, no lines. No role. My heart sank. I was nothing more than a song-and-dance man—a German song-and-dance man.

I could feel myself losing perspective. This was an original Broadway role. Most actors worked their whole lives without ever getting that kind of opportunity. I was crazy even to question it. But what if this wasn't *really* a role? Being so peripheral in a high-profile production might solidify a reputation as a featured player. I got myself so twisted up that I didn't know what to think, so I took the script into the kitchen where Jo was reading a magazine and having a snack. Looking up at me, thin-lipped and gripping the pages, she could immediately see that I was upset.

The Epsteins: Morris and Fanny;
"The Sisters" Helen, Grace, Esther, and
Frida (Fritzi). Baby Beverly was born later.

The Katz family: Max, Abe, Mama
Johanna, Jeanne, Estelle, and
Myron (Mickey).

Photo booth shot of the folks
(circa 1930s).

Dad, one- or two-year-old me, and Mom at
"Mother's Camp" in Ohio.

"Learning the ropes" from The Scarecrow, Ray Bolger (1940s).

The four of us: "The Katz Family Robinson."

With Rock Hudson on location in Rome
for *Come September* in 1961.

Maverick Jim Garner and me as
"Billy the Kid."

Harry Belafonte and me.

In his dressing room in Munich.

Me with my darling Bernadette Peters
in *George M!*

Goodtime Charley, 1975: as
"The Dauphin."

James, Jennifer, and me vacationing on Nantucket, 1973.

Backstage at The Riviera, Las Vegas with legends Liza and Ann Margret.

Judy Garland (OMG) in my dressing room at the Palace, 1967, after *George M!*

Me with Kermit on the *The Muppet Show.*

With Agnes Gund and Philip Johnson, Municipal Art Society's "Honorary New Yorkers," 1983.

Banner outside the Museum of the City of New York for my photo exhibit *A New York Life* in 2011.

A historic staged reading I directed of *The Normal Heart* in 2010 at The Walter Kerr Theatre in New York City. *Back row, from left:* Joe Mantello, Larry Kramer, Jason Butler Harner, Victor Garber, Jack McBrayer, John Benjamin Hickey, and Patrick Wilson; *front row, from left:* Glenn Close, me, Michael Stuhlbarg, Michael Cerveris, and Santino Fontana.

Clark, Jennifer, and Stella Gregg, 2015.

James, now a first-rate chef, and me
on holiday in Bermuda.

Always close.

Jennifer and me at the Tony Awards, 2015.

"Wonderful" Idina Menzel
and me in *Wicked*, 2003.

"Honey, could you take a few minutes and please read this," I asked.

She took the script into our bedroom, closed the door, and reappeared forty minutes later, walking straight at me and giving me a huge hug. "This is a fantastic script and a daring concept," she said. "And you will be amazing in it."

Jo had insight into matters of the theater and was rarely wrong. I trusted her above anyone else and needed to remember how smart she always was about these things.

"I don't think there is a decision here," she said.

We agreed I would do it, and so it was that I found myself ambivalent and a little apprehensive beginning rehearsals for *Cabaret*. As if the fact I didn't have any lines wasn't clear enough from the script, rehearsals were bizarrely split up between the dancers and the actors. In a wholly unconventional plan, Hal rehearsed as if there were two shows. The book scenes were rehearsed at the theater with the cast that included Jill Haworth as Sally Bowles; Bert Convy, as her lover, Clff; Jack Gilford as Herr Schultz; and in the part of Fräulein Schneider, Lotte Lenya, Brecht's widow, who had appeared in *The Threepenny Opera* with Jo and attended our wedding. Meanwhile, I (in a tailcoat with satin lapels frayed from use that the costume designer Patricia Zipprodt and I had picked out at the Brooks Costume Company) rehearsed the musical numbers with the ensemble at a midtown studio. It felt a little like being seated at the children's table.

I worked with the choreographer, Ron Field, who had a brilliantly elegant and sleazy take on the musical numbers. The veteran dancer Michel Stuart was also on hand to help with my tap dancing, although it was minimal. Still, something was missing. As rehearsals continued, my isolation from the actors in the play fueled my initial insecurity. I let it reinforce my constant worry that I didn't belong. I fixated on the fact that I didn't feel like an actor at all instead of accepting the real problem: I hadn't found the character. Sardonic and dark songs didn't tell me anything about the Emcee. I had no idea what I was doing. Meanwhile, somewhere between hearing the score at John's and the start of rehearsal, the creative team changed their minds about the one big Act 2 production number (all six songs) and decided to intersperse them throughout the show.

The challenge was to seduce the audience into having a good time, just as Hitler excited the German people into genocide. The Emcee was grotesque *and* seductive. The musical numbers were there to subliminally comment on the book scenes, and the Emcee was a musical dictator, if you will, representing Hitler's seduction of the Germans. I bade the audience to join me in the fun and kept them waiting with baited breath for my return. Only at the end would I reveal they had been duped. But how was I to do that in any kind of convincing way if the Emcee remained an enigma even to me? I needed to find the psychological nature of the Emcee. He needed to be a real person with a backstory and aspirations. I had struggled with the decision to do *Cabaret* precisely because I feared that I wouldn't be able to find anything deeper than a nightclub performer. With every passing day of rehearsal my fear seemed to become more of a reality.

Then, a couple of weeks before the show's out-of-town tryout in Boston, inspiration came from the most unlikely of places—the vile comedian I had seen perform in St. Louis when I was on the nightclub circuit and had reappeared in my dreams while I rehearsed for *Cabaret*. These two men—the Emcee and the comedian in my dreams—were one and the same: both totally corrupt, desperate for adoration, willing to do anything to save themselves. And so finally, armed with the motivation that had thus far eluded me, I *became* the comedian while Hal watched from his seat in the auditorium. I groped, ogled, and played the buffoon, catching the rest of the ensemble—and myself— off guard. Afterward, I raced offstage in shame, appalled that I had access to such a sleazy creep. But Hal was ecstatic. Talk about a breakthrough! It had taken me so long to "find" the Emcee because all my life he was who I never wanted to be. I'd seen his like from almost my earliest days of performing, and vowed never to be that.

Finally knowing who I was, I came up with an elaborate biography. I decided where he lived in Berlin and what his flat looked like; I knew he would force the Kit Kat Klub girls to have sex with him in his dressing room in payment for giving them the job. Men could also find favor with him through sex. The Emcee wasn't just bisexual, he was any-and-every-sexual. Something I played with was the question of whether he in fact was Jewish. I never told anyone any of these details; they were strictly for me.

Next the Emcee needed a look. The man Hal had seen while in the service wore the sort of makeup a transvestite might. But we found that women's products—base, rouge, lipstick, lashes—just didn't work. My character was androgynous, not trying to pass as a woman. For me, he existed on two levels as a real, flesh-and-blood "second rater" in a tacky cabaret, and also the symbol of decadence. I needed to make him both highly specific and iconic.

I plundered Jo's makeup case, which was full of old European makeup from her early days acting in summer stock. I searched out each color and texture, the way I imagine a painter does when starting with a blank canvas. In front of my wife's vanity, I was transported back to the nine-year-old boy sitting in the dressing room of the Cleveland Play House watching with fascination as the older actors put on beards, mustaches, wigs, shading, and putty to create their characters. Only now I was the older actor, too.

I started with a stick called juvenile pink (the Emcee would want to look younger), matted down with Johnson's baby powder. I then drew thick, dark, slightly arched eyebrows and dark orange underbrows, and layered blue eye shadow on the lids. Jo's old lashes were so thick with mascara that they looked like black construction paper or the lashes of a ventriloquist's dummy. Perfect. I applied raspberry rouge to my cheeks, and for the lips, not a lipstick (no shade looked right) but a type of old German shading stick called Leichner's "lake." I parted my hair in the center and flattened it against my skull with Dippity-do. I looked in the mirror, and there he was, "Willkommen! Bienvenue! Welcome!"

Everyone involved in the show seemed inspired; something special was in the air. John's score was brilliant, Fred's lyrics evocative. Joe's story looked unflinchingly at taboo topics while still managing to remain funny. Ron Field choreographed the Kit Kat Klub girls ("each and every one a virgin") and me with evil charm. Boris Aronson—the son of a rabbi who got his start as a Tony Award–winning scenic designer making sets for the Yiddish theater—made the members of the audience complicit in the action by having them face their reflection in a large mirror placed near the vanishing point of the stage. And I brought the character of the Emcee, who turned out to be not only the glue but also the essence of the show.

The Emcee's musical numbers—such as "Two Ladies"—are very specifically placed into the show to let us know that there are no limits in a world that is about to descend into chaos. But the Emcee also brings the alluring, prurient world of the Kit Kat Klub from the very opening of the show. Leave your troubles outside! The importance of transporting the audience to Weimar Germany, which has never stopped being a point of curiosity, cannot be overstated. It is one of the crucial elements to the show's enduring appeal.

Opening night at the Shubert Theatre in Boston, however, we had no idea how the audience was going to receive the show. Of course, we were all anxious. Musical theater is such a fragile form. Making one work is an epic undertaking, and here we were singing and dancing about Nazism. Did the kind of person who went out to the theater to see a musical really want to deal with such complex and disturbing topics? Suddenly, it seemed crazy to think so.

Any last-minute doubts, however, were dispelled by the audience's thunderous reaction to the opening number. They applauded, shouted, practically stood up from their seats! The applause went on so long that the opening number literally stopped the show. Backstage, the cast wandered around startled and confused, asking one another, "What should we do?" "Should we go out and do it again?" "How long do you wait?"

As the Emcee, I was confrontational, using my bamboo cane as if it were an extension of my randy, roving arms, or maybe a weapon to not so gently teach the girls a lesson. Despite the dark, bizarre atmosphere of Berlin, I promised the audience a good time. "In here, life is beautiful. The girls are beautiful. Even the orchestra is beautiful." And the members of the audience, titillated during "Two Ladies," were happy to become my accomplices.

"We switch partners daily / To play as we please," I sang with two girls.

"Twosie beats Onesie," sang Girl One.

"But nothing beats threes," I'd sing and wait a beat before going on: "I sleep in the middle."

"I'm left," sang Girl One. "Und I'm right," added Girl Two.

"But there's room on the bottom," I'd continue, looking at the crowd, "if you drop in some night.

The audience happily accepted our invitation to a ménage with the lyric. Through all of Act 1, the onlookers trusted that life was indeed beautiful, because I was their friend—until I wasn't.

The first knife went in at the very end of the first act during a party scene when Fräulein Kost (played by Peg Murray who also won a Tony that year) reprised the song "Tomorrow Belongs to Me," which had earlier in the show been performed innocently by the waiters of the Kit Kat Klub. The song, which began sweetly with a melody John had invented, based on traditional German folk music, grew in force as the orchestra joined in—just as Fred's lyrics, which had started bucolically ("The branch on the linden is leafy and green / The Rhine gives its gold to the sea") turned nationalistic and menacing ("Fatherland, Fatherland, show us the sign / Your children have waited to see"). But if the audience didn't understand the true meaning of the party-goers' rendition, when Fräulein Kost performed it she was joined by Ernst proudly wearing a swastika on his sleeve. That was the sharpening of the blade, which I stuck in when walking across the stage as the Emcee, I looked directly at the audience and whispered, "Tomorrow belongs to . . . me." Blackout.

What have we been doing? What have we been watching? Who is this character that we thought was fun, and amusing, and smart and witty? All these thoughts were running through the heads of the theatergoers, who when the houselights came up were left staring at themselves in the mirror on stage.

For the start of Act 2, I needed to make it my mission to get them laughing and having fun again, no easy feat considering where we had left them so abruptly before the lights went out. I hid among the Kit Kat Girls, who came out in a kickline. When the audience discovered me in the line, in drag, it was a big surprise. And like that the people in their seats were shocked, surprised, and back on my side.

But they didn't have long before I jammed in the second knife. Performing the number "If You Could See Her," I professed my love for a "girl" gorilla (there was actually a man inside the costume) and exhorted the audience—again, my friends—to accept our union. "If you could see her through my eyes," I sang, "she wouldn't look Jewish at all." Not a sound, let alone a laugh, from the audience as the deed was done.

On opening night at the Broadhurst Theatre, November 20, 1966, I was emboldened by three weeks of previews, in which the audiences were screaming with horror and delight. That night, however, I got an extra boost from friends and colleagues who had rooted for me over the years. Opening night wires poured in from everywhere: Mom and Dad, Aunt Jeannie, and Cousin Burton. Even K. Elmo Lowe sent one: "Good luck, Mr. Katz. I know you'll be wonderful. STOP. Don't wiggle." My favorite, however, came from my friend Buck Henry, the comedy writer and actor: "Wish I were there to observe your peculiar ways."

Wearing the very same tailcoat Patricia and I originally chose for rehearsal and an equally worn-out dirty pink vest, I was never more peculiar than that night. Through hard work, not only in *Cabaret* but every performance I had ever given, I found the character that one could not deny.

This is what I had dreamt about, struggled for, worked hard at, and, oh, my God, here it was!

CHAPTER TEN

The nightclub career I had tried so hard to overcome was the very thing I drew upon to find the low vaudevillian that was the Emcee. As much as I fought against being a song-and-dance man, it was during those smoke-filled nights at the Chez, the Copa, and even the dreaded Town Casino in snowy Buffalo, where I was heckled, that the Emcee's utter smiling soullessness was born.

At thirty-four, *Cabaret* changed my life. In his review of the show for the *New York Times*, Walter Kerr, who was no fan of the original play *I Am a Camera* (his review's headline: ME NO LEICA), raved about *Cabaret* and my work: "Master of Ceremonies Joel Grey bursts from the darkness like a tracer bullet . . . cheerful, charming, soulless and conspiratorially wicked."

Cabaret also experienced, not surprisingly, some controversy. It centered on the lyric "She wouldn't look *Jewish* at all," in the number "If You Could See Her (The Gorilla Song)." During previews, some Jewish groups, totally misunderstanding its true significance, opposed the last line, the punch line in the show. They thought it, in and of itself, was anti-Semitic, instead of it in fact being an ironic comment on anti-Semitism! Their protests became so emphatic that Hal decided rather than endanger the life of the whole show, during previews I was to replace the original line with "She isn't a meeskite at all." Meeskite—Yiddish for *ugly* or *funny-looking*—was supposed to deliver the same meaning! The change took some of the teeth out of the ugly punchline in the show, but the audience got the point. My job was to make the audience know they had been betrayed. After we opened, there were nights when I spontaneously slipped "look Jewish" back in, prompting the stage manager to scream at me, "What are you doing?" "Shit," I would say, smiling, "I forgot!"

The set, costumes, staging, and music were so compelling and original that they kept *Cabaret* running for 1,165 performances.

When the show opened, I started out with fifth-featured billing but was ultimately moved up to fourth—an event that was marked by a party held at the Ground Floor, the cool restaurant done to William Paley's tasteful specifications at the base of the CBS Building. Every actor on Broadway turned up. The party was a surprise, but so was the success of the Emcee. It wasn't anyone's plan for my character to become the focal point of the show. *Cabaret*'s story centered on Sally Bowles and Cliff Bradshaw. I was just a metaphor, and nobody expected the metaphor to become the centerpiece.

Cabaret made me a celebrity. When Joan Crawford came to the show, she asked to meet me. So while I was still in my makeup, I heard a knock on the door and then in walked one of the greatest screen legends of all time. Heavily made up with large, black, penciled-in eyebrows, her silver hair in a high coif, and many strands of large pearls winding around her neck, she looked like a drag version of Joan Crawford. Very grand, but she couldn't have been nicer. Her husband, Al Steele, all business in his gray double-breasted suit, accompanied her, the straight man to her star. They arrived without fanfare and exchanged the normal backstage pleasantries ("You were great . . ."). But having the iconic Joan Crawford come backstage to meet me symbolized the unprecedented success that I was to experience with *Cabaret*.

It even changed my relationship with Mother. Years ago, whenever I went out shopping with her, or wherever she dragged me when I visited LA, she was always quick to announce to storekeepers, restaurant owners, and the like, "I'm Mrs. Mickey Katz." After my success in *Cabaret*, however, I noticed that she changed the line: "I'm Joel Grey's mother! I'm Grace!"

Jo and I became the new "it kids" and were invited to all of these fancy events. On Monday nights, my night off from the show, we often found ourselves at swanky parties with people I knew more from the press than from real life. One evening was an intimate dinner at Café des Artistes, at which Mayor John Lindsay was seated to my left; another was a big fund-raiser at the Waldorf with celebrity chefs such as Marcella Hazan, from whom I had taken an Italian cooking class. (Twice a week, six of us in her kitchen in her apartment on Lexington Avenue spent all morning cooking her recipes, which we ate for lunch. It was sublime and very serious. I learned her classic tomato sauce, which I still make today.)

Jennifer, who was six years old at the time, also got a taste of glamour when she would come to visit me at the theater during weekend matinee performances. Dressed up special, she would sit in my dressing room watching me intently as I got made up. The chorus girls always made a tremendous fuss over Jennifer, who had good manners and the ability to hold her own with adults. They would make her up like a Kit Kat Girl, much to her delight. But when it came time for the production to start, Jennifer quietly stood in the wings to watch just as I had watched my father at the RKO in Cleveland. The rituals of the theater became a part of Jennifer, who always loved dancing around the apartment dressed up in costumes made from odds and ends I had collected for her from various shows over the years—including the Kit Kat Girl headband with a black velvet cat face.

The press took a new interest in me. *Women's Wear Daily* did a style piece and *Vogue* ran a full-page Milton Greene photo of me surrounded by the Kit Kat Girls. They were also interested in Jo, who as a style setter in designer clothing by Rudi Gernreich, Halston, and Gustave Tassell, was covered by fashion magazines. Jo was thrilled with the attention. My success was hers. Very literally, I owed her a debt of gratitude for having persuaded me to stay the course and take the part of the Emcee when I had my doubts. But even more, Jo was part of the fabric of the play. As a performer, she understood all its nuances, and she had been a dear friend of Lenya's before I knew either of them. When I wore Jo's makeup from summer stock, it was like a part of her was up on stage, too.

Even our apartment got press. THE EASY-GOING COSMOS OF A STAR, read the headline of an article about our place in *House & Garden*. "Behind the Joel Greys' discreet brass doorplate is an apartment filled with all the gaiety of a triumphant opening night." The hype! The apartment, into which we had moved at Central Park West and 87th Street, was indeed spacious. The front apartment belonged to the actress Shelley Winters, of course facing the park. Befitting "Broadway's newest and brightest comedy star," as *House & Garden* hilariously dubbed me, the apartment was done by Albert Hadley, who we met through Hal and Judy Prince. He had designed interiors for the biggest names in America from Rockefeller to Kennedy. Sherbet-pink, apple-green, and bright paisley furniture stood in contrast to white walls, zebra rugs, and parquet floors. It was all very uptown—still, Jo and I retained a little Village bohemianism with our quilt-covered brass bed.

The single most meaningful excitement during that period, however, was *Cabaret*'s being nominated for eleven Tony Awards in 1967—including one for me. The 21st Annual Tony Awards ceremony, held at the Shubert Theatre, opened with "Willkommen." Not only was I performing for an audience of the greats, my heroes in the theater, but, for the first time in the Tonys' history, the award show was going to be broadcast live in prime time. When we rehearsed the number on the day of the show, everyone was very, very nervous—including me.

On top of the anxiety about the live TV performance, I worried about whether I was going to win. I knew I had a good chance. Still!!

I don't know how the rest of the country watching the Tonys felt, but inside the Shubert Theatre that night, the Broadway audience wholeheartedly embraced this little musical about Nazis, anti-Semitism, and homosexuals. *Cabaret* won eight Tonys, including Best Musical, Best Original Score, Best Choreography, and, for me, Best Featured Actor in a Musical.

When the famous husband-and-wife dance team Marge and Gower Champion opened the envelope and she said my name, I bounded from the back of the theater toward the stage with all the energy of the eight-year-old Pud at the Cleveland Play House. This is what I had dreamt about, struggled for, worked hard at, and, oh, my God, here it was! After first kissing my beautiful wife, I leapt onto the stage to thank every-one who had helped me get here, ending with "Danke schön. Merci. Thank you. Thank you."

So I accepted the role of George M. Cohan—yet another
song-and-dance man, although one of mythic proportions.

CHAPTER ELEVEN

Winning a Tony meant more dinner invitations and press, but most important, it led to my first starring role on Broadway, while still playing the Emcee. Again without requiring an audition, I was offered the title role in the musical *George M!*, which was based on the life of George M. Cohan. The *Cabaret* producers were less than thrilled about my leaving the show after my yearlong contract was up, and I had my own conflicts about the decision as well.

Playing the Emcee had always been a satisfying experience. It was never less than exciting eight times a week. Not only was the production of such a high caliber, but as a Jew I also believed strongly in the important political message it relayed. Having birthed that character, it became a part of me. So the idea of my understudy taking it over felt strange and sad—kind of like leaving your child for someone else to take care of. But I was ready to take on the next challenge, and Jo supported me in that; she wanted me to continue to succeed and stretch myself. So I accepted the role of Cohan—yet another song-and-dance man, although one of mythic proportions.

Both the script and the concept behind *George M!* were terrific. The hard-driving performer, who never wore makeup and called everyone kid, was probably the most famous composer in the American songbook, even though he knew only four chords in the key of F-sharp.

The director, Joe Layton, and Michael Stewart, who wrote the book along with Fran Pascal, Mike's sister, had a fresh approach to the real Cohan story that was challenging and risky. James Cagney had played Cohan wonderfully in *Yankee Doodle Dandy*, but as was the Hollywood habit, the film avoided the darker aspects of his life such as his anti-union positions and the heavy hand he took with his family. Mike's version showed the dictatorial and temperamental side of the man who had written more than fifty plays and such beloved songs as "Give My Regards to Broadway" and "Over There."

Then there was the style of the book. The form was impressionistic, with a unique set that gave suggestions of place instead of being conventionally realistic. Time passed very quickly from episode to episode of Cohan's life, with only slight changes in costume signaling the transitions. Rather than being dressed fully in period clothing, the actors would start the play in contemporary clothing, and for each song a piece of period attire would be added, maybe an apron, hat, or vest.

I very much liked the complexity of this dark version. The only problem was that I worried I was wrong for the part. First there was the matter of Cohan's Irish Catholic background. But if I could play an evil Nazi Emcee, I was hoping I could play Irish. More worrying was the idea of singing Cohan's classics, and the most daunting of all was getting an audience to believe I was a superb tap dancer like Cohan—or for that matter, Cagney, who was also a phenomenal hoofer. All I'd had were a couple of months of lessons when I was a kid back in Cleveland. I thought of my initial worries about the part of the Emcee and how deeply satisfying and transformative an experience playing that character was. But I would never know what I was capable of if I didn't try.

So after a year on Broadway in the season's biggest hit, we took a quick vacation at Frenchman's Cove in Jamaica (where it rained the entire week) and then went straight into rehearsal for *George M!* Joe Layton was a relentless and brilliant taskmaster, and the choreography was extremely complex, even for experienced tappers. The style of tap dancing Layton wanted wasn't the Fred Astaire and Gene Kelly variety but a hybrid with Irish clog dancing that made it uniquely off-kilter and fresh. And he was very exacting about its execution.

The biggest challenge in learning to dance like Cohan wasn't his style of dancing but the fact that he was the *best* tap dancer of his time. I began a crash course in tap with Bob Audy, the best teacher in New York, with a great assist from Layton's right-hand man, Wakefield Poole. Every day I would walk over to his studio on Broadway not far from home and go through the basic exercises of tap. I did shuffle flaps, stomp rolls, and every other dance step until I was soaking wet. It took tremendous energy to do the basic steps over and over, but I couldn't move on to combinations until I had mastered them.

After my work with Bob, who gave me so much confidence, I headed downtown to rehearse the book scenes and musical numbers for hours. This was a show where I was onstage for all but one number. During the endless and exhausting process, there wasn't a day that went by when I didn't wonder if they had hired the wrong guy. But there was no quitting. I'd signed my name to the show. They were putting up the marquee, with my name over the title, at the Palace Theatre, where I had seen Judy Garland and Danny Kaye's names in lights. Opposite the theater, a statue of George M. Cohan himself kept watch as if to say, "Don't mess this up, kid." A lot of money was on the line, and a bunch of my wonderful and talented fellow actors were depending on me.

One of those was Bernadette Peters, who immediately nailed the part of Cohan's younger sister, Josie, the minute she opened her mouth. It was startling when this young, adorably young girl sang; no one had ever heard a sound like that. We all fell in love with her immediately.

Where there were about five or six actors being considered for every part, no one could compete with Bernadette; she *was* Josie.

She was a show-business kid who grew up in Queens in a Sicilian family. Her mother, tough and always around, was a real stage mom (albeit a likable one) who put her talented daughter on TV at the age of three and a half. By the time she was thirteen, Bernadette had become an understudy in a national tour of *Gypsy*. She and I got along immediately, and I quickly became a safe retreat when her mother was driving her crazy, which was often. I knew from mothers.

Everyone involved loved the show, and we were pretty confident when we headed to Detroit for the out-of-town tryout. All of the investors and producers came in from New York as well. The first upset: A newspaper strike was going on, which meant no reviews and lower ticket sales. And as if that weren't unlucky enough, a historic snowstorm covered the city. As a result the Fisher Theatre looked like a half-empty school auditorium when the curtain opened.

There were many times I regretted leaving *Cabaret*; many, many times. But no more so than in that moment: facing an empty theater in the middle of an epic snowstorm in Detroit. It wasn't lost on me that I could have been the toast of London, since a production of *Cabaret* opened in England while the original still ran on Broadway.

The situation went from bad to worse as the audience that braved the weather was less than thrilled with *George M!* Even in the cavernous space of the Fisher Theatre I could feel the tepid response as we knocked ourselves out. The loose style of the show that I had found compelling proved too abstract—arty, even. So there we were, a big, brassy out-of-town musical in trouble.

After the performance, Joe, Mike, my agent and great friend Sam Cohn, and the rest of the creative team and producers had what was reported to be a long meeting at their hotel, the results of which would yield the next step in "fixing the show." They all agreed that what was missing were fleshed out production numbers of the Cohan biggies, such as "Yankee Doodle Dandy." So the plan was to rethink and restage most of Act 2 to give the iconic songs their full due. Of course, in order to do this, other material would have to be cut—actors might lose their only big moment. The next day, there were frayed nerves all around. Everyone was exhausted, but we had to push on, rehearsing for most of the day, stopping for a quick bite and a nap, then back to the theater for an eight-thirty curtain.

Of course, narcissist that I was, I thought everything was my fault. For eight performances a week, I rarely left the stage, and for as many hours as the union would allow, we rehearsed a gigantic new twenty-minute production number for Act 2 that had all-new choreography to accomplish these fully realized versions of "Over There," "Nellie Kelly, I Love You," "Harrigan," "You're a Grand Old Flag," and "Yankee Doodle Dandy." Expensive new costumes were made and new set pieces built, all of which would hopefully guide the audience more explicitly and conventionally through the great man's life story. The big question that hung over the show as we came to a close in Detroit was whether the changes, as big and costly and exhausting as they were, would turn it around.

As we got closer to opening night of *George M!*, I was anxious even though the Detroit audiences seemed to like the show more with the new additions. I had just come off a big hit that some said had changed the shape of American musicals. This time, with my name above the title, if the show failed, it could put a hard stop to my momentum. It's not unusual to blame the actor.

Many Broadway musicals, even those created by icons such as Richard Rodgers, Josh Logan, Irving Berlin, and Leonard Bernstein, have struggled out of town, giving their talented all to "fix a show," only to have it ultimately fail on Broadway. The best of them, Michael Bennett, Hal Prince, Bob Fosse, Jerome Robbins, have all had this experience at one time or another. That's one of the reasons why musical theater is so completely thrilling when it does work.

The substantive changes to the material went very well at the Shubert Theater in Philadelphia, our second out-of-town run before coming to New York. Before the curtain went up, everyone onstage held hands like a family. After prayers and other preshow necessities, the lights went up, and from that instant, the audience plain loved it. They erupted with applause and laughter at every turn. It was pretty clear from the standing ovation we received at the end of the show that the flashy new MGM-style musical numbers had done the trick.

Fifty minutes before the curtain was scheduled to go up at New York's Palace Theatre, on April 10, 1968, I headed out of my dressing room before putting on my costume. Amid the mayhem of opening night on Broadway, hardly anyone noticed as I made my way along the row of dressing rooms, down the stairs, past the orchestra's pit, and under the stage, where I found myself alone, in the half light of a ghost light. I put on my tap shoes and ran through the very demanding solo in the show's first number, "All Aboard for Broadway."

I was terrified of blowing my first tap solo. The long and complicated sequence would have been challenging for any tap dancer. For a novice like me, it was truly scary. On top of that, I was about to perform it in a theater that contained the likes of Henry Fonda, Albert Finney, and Cohan's daughter Georgette. I needed to run through my solo one last time before the curtain went up to make sure the steps were still "in my feet."

My feet didn't forget, and the opening was gangbusters. Practicing a half hour before curtain under the stage with the ghost light became my ritual for every single show during the entire run. The opening night party, which happened to be on my birthday, was held at the Plaza Hotel. One of our producers, Konrad Matthaei and his wife, Gay, hosted the red-white-and-blue-themed event attended by theater, business, and society elites Gloria Vanderbilt and her fourth husband, Wyatt Cooper; Henri Bendel president Gerry Stutz; and Liza Minnelli and Peter Allen. Men in black tie and women, who had been asked to wear red, white, and blue, danced to music provided by the renowned bandleader Peter Duchin and his orchestra. To me, no one there looked more beautiful than Jo Wilder Grey in a heavy ridged white cotton dress made for her by designer Gus Tassell. The dress was so simple and devoid of decoration (even the buttons were hidden under a fly front) that it reminded me of the gown she wore on our wedding day.

There was much cause for celebration—*George M!* felt like a big hit. But as it turned out, there was a general perception of the show as jingoistic. In 1968, an antiwar time, many people dismissed our show's message as naive patriotism and not the dark cautionary tale about a brilliant but deeply flawed artist that it was.

The burgeoning politically radical era was only part of the problem. Despite all the revisions, the reviews were still not great. In the *New York Times* on April 11 (my birthday), Clive Barnes called the show "ill-prepared" and "mediocrely written." However, he did praise my performance: "[Joel Grey] sang lightly and beltingly, he danced, with frenetic passion and a God-given sense of timing, and when all else failed, he even acted the script that they had been inconsiderate enough to give him."

Not everyone, however, liked my performance. I was devastated when ten days after Barnes's review, Walter Kerr skewered me in a big Sunday piece in the *Times*. In the article, humiliatingly titled YANKEE DOODLE'S OUT OF BREATH, Kerr went on for paragraphs and paragraphs. "Mr. Grey does not ask for a rest, though we do," wrote the very same man who in *Cabaret* said I was the sun, moon, and stars.

I didn't know what to do. I remembered what my father used to always say about critics; if they don't like your show, audiences won't either—because the show will no longer be running. Certainly having Walter Kerr lay into me in the Sunday *Times* could close a show. Jo, who saw me in a panic after I read the review, tried to lighten the situation with a more realistic and levelheaded perspective.

"This is just one man's opinion," she said. "You are wonderful and the audience loves it."

"But it's the *whole* page of the Sunday *Times*."

"How about what Clive Barnes said? He raved about your performance."

"Walter Kerr is more respected."

There was nothing Jo could say that was going to make me feel better. I picked up the phone and called my great good friend Beverly Sills, the great soprano. She was not only smart but had a lot of experience dealing with the ups and downs of the press during her long, high-profile career. (A few years later, she landed the cover of *Time* with the cover line AMERICA'S QUEEN OF OPERA.)

"Is this the end of my career?" I asked Beverly.

"There will be a million of those articles," she said. "Just forget it. It's part of being on top. They want to pull you down."

Of course she knew of what she spoke, but I was never able to stop reading reviews. I'm ashamed to admit that over the years I came to fret irrationally about the press. There was something masochistic, even counterproductive to my worrying: It served only to erode my self-confidence and not improve the work in any way. There are so many people who never read reviews, and I applaud them. However, whenever I didn't read them my imagination would run wild, conjuring up fantasy reviews that were far worse than anything anyone had written.

I was thankful that people in my life such as Beverly were there during tough times. I was in one of those down-on-myself states when, while exiting the stage door after a performance, I ran into the husband-and-wife theater legends and longtime collaborators Ruth Gordon and Garson Kanin, who had just been to the matinee. They were standing on the corner of 47th and Broadway, going on about how much they loved my work. But feeling tired and low, which was pretty much how I felt daily, I said, "I don't know. I think whatever I had, maybe it's gone."

Ruth, who had recently won an Academy Award for her unforgettable role in Roman Polanski's *Rosemary's Baby*, looked me in the face and said with steely conviction, "Once you are an artist, you're always an artist." I have returned to those words often over the years for support.

In the end it wasn't reviews that closed *George M!* but rather President Richard Nixon. He had brought Pat and their daughters, Tricia and Julie, to see the show, and he of course came backstage to congratulate the cast on a job well done. I didn't want to have my picture taken with him, but I had no choice—and that photo of the two of us, along with Nixon's personal approval of the show, was wildly publicized. He was as unpleasant-looking in real life as he was on TV and even his compliments made one feel uneasy. Normally when the president of the United States comes to see a Broadway show, the excitement extends the run. Not with Nixon. As if selling Broadway on a musical filled with patriotic tunes during the late sixties weren't hard enough, Nixon had to stick his unpopular face in my very own dressing room.

New Yorkers might have felt that they were too hip for the Cohan music, but the rest of the country could hardly wait to hear that great American songbook. I followed in the footsteps of some of Broadway's greatest stars—such as Ethel Merman, Mary Martin, and Alfred Drake—who typically toured with their shows after the run in New York was done. While *Cabaret* continued to run, the six-month national tour of *George M!* was one of the biggest grossers on the road at that time. In places such as Cleveland, Houston, and Denver, we were constantly sold out and cheered. We even played to mostly sold-out audiences at the Music Center in Los Angeles for ten weeks over the summer.

I was grateful that Jo and the children came out to join me in LA, where we rented a swell house on Beverly Drive. In an interview with the *Oakland Tribune* from June 21, 1969, Jo described the idyllic mixture of work and family life that allowed us to all have dinner together at 5:30 P.M. before I showered, shaved, rested, and left for the theater. Jo explained how she had started to turn down roles when my career took off.

"I don't know how husbands and wives can be in the same profession, pushing in opposite directions," Jo told the reporter. "They are rare people who can do this without becoming estranged from each other. Joel was never really happy when I was working, so I just quit, and I'm much happier now."

I loved seeing that those were her words. I had made good on those very early promises to take care of her and make her proud and safe. We had come a long way from the days when we had fought about her having a career, and I felt that my success had finally become our success.

Academy Award - 1972
Best Supporting Actor.
"Cabaret."

Don't let anybody tell you this isn't a big thrill.

rarely read the trades anymore, but while in the waiting room of my dentist's office, I picked up *Variety,* where I saw the latest news: Ruth Gordon had met with Bob Fosse regarding playing the Emcee in the upcoming Allied Artists film *Cabaret.*

What?

After five years of deliberation, a movie version of *Cabaret* had finally been green-lighted, which set off a flurry of rumors that had been flying for weeks. Cy Feuer and Ernie Martin, famous for their Broadway blockbusters, such as *Guys and Dolls* and *How to Succeed in Business Without Really Trying,* were producing for Marty Baum's company under the aegis of Manny Wolf and ABC Pictures.

A lot of changes were being made for the film version. Fosse, the director, wanted to stay as far away from the stage musical as possible in order to put his personal stamp on *Cabaret.*

Major structural changes to the story were being made by Jay Presson Allen and Hugh Wheeler, who were writing the script. All the songs that were sung as part of the more conventional Broadway musical were cut; in the film, characters would never speak and then sing to one another as stage and film musicals had always been done. That old-fashioned style had fallen out of favor. It was also decided that the numbers in the Kit Kat Klub (including some new songs by the original team John Kander and Fred Ebb, such as "Money, Money" and "Mein Herr") should exist in real time and in a real club for a realistic musical film dealing with drastic world consequences.

No one from the original play was set to appear in the film. Liza Minnelli was a great choice for Sally Bowles, and Michael York was set to play Brian, a stand-in for Christopher Isherwood, her gay lover (as opposed to the stage version, in which the character was decidedly heterosexual). That was appropriate, since the original character in the short story "Welcome to Berlin," by the openly gay Christopher Isherwood, was autobiographical. Marisa Berenson, the exquisite model and actress, was to play a new character, Natalia Landauer, the Jewish department-store heiress. That character filled the place that was left after Lotte Lenya's character, Fräulein Schneider, had been cut. And to round it out, a young suitor, Fritz, supposedly Gentile, falls in love with Natalia, and their story line is intertwined with the rise of the Nazis and anti-Semitism in Berlin.

Just as he recast all the other original roles, Bob adamantly wanted someone new to play the Emcee. So I wasn't surprised to read in *Variety* that he was looking at other actors for the part—but Ruth Gordon? She would certainly bring a totally different slant to the part. Another top contender was Anthony Newley, whose agent, Sue Mengers, was pitching very hard for the role.

I couldn't imagine someone else inhabiting the Emcee on the big screen, a character that would remain in the popular imagination long after the memory of a theater performance had faded.

Sam Cohn, Bob's agent and mine, was in a very awkward spot.

"You know how it goes," Sam said, trying to keep it light. "At first, they always try to reinvent the wheel. There's always the period where they go through the 'Is Clint Eastwood available?' or 'What if we offer it to Kirk Douglas?'"

But I knew it was (and still is) a director's medium. They usually have the power, and even though his previous film, *Sweet Charity*, had gone over budget and hadn't done well at the box office, he was still the great multiple-Tony-winning Bob Fosse.

But six weeks before preproduction was set to begin in Munich, they still hadn't settled on an Emcee!

A summit was arranged in Marty Baum's office at Allied with the entire producing team. As I was told by Marty many years later at a dinner party, the meeting had been called because he and the other producers wanted me for the part. But Bob, playing hardball, wouldn't relent. He thought that if push came to shove, they wouldn't get rid of the director for the sake of an actor.

Bob entered the meeting and announced, "I guess this is the moment of truth. It's either Joel Grey or me!"

Without hesitation, Marty said, "Then it's Joel Grey."

The part was mine, but what a start to my working relationship with the director! The first time I saw Bob in our new roles was right before we left for Germany. We met at a rehearsal studio to go over some ideas for the numbers. Bob was a lot older than when I had first met him in 1950, performing a nightclub act, Fosse and Niles, with his then wife, Mary Ann Niles. But today he seemed just as remote as ever. Two assistants flanked him. Despite the chilly reception, I was a professional and put my most charming self forward. The only thing that came out of his mouth was smoke from the cigarette always hanging out of it.

So we skipped the pleasantries and went to work.

I was three bars into the song when he stopped me.

"Hold it," he said to the pianist. "Let's start again."

I started again, and just as quickly was stopped.

"Why are you moving the rest of your body?" he asked. "I want to see *hands*."

As the director and choreographer, Bob had the right to ask anything, but his direction had an edge to it. He demonstrated a couple of bars so that I could see what he meant. Bob's style was very specific and recognizable. He was a huge fan of jazz hands. Very often every word had a move assigned to it. He never expected improvisation and wanted every muscle choreographed to counts. But I wasn't sure about some of his ideas for these numbers. The highly stylized moves didn't feel right.

I kept on starting, and he kept on stopping me. I tried to do what he asked even if I thought it was dead wrong. We found ourselves at an impasse. Bob stood there, arms crossed and smoking, closed off and combative. Meanwhile, I continued to ignore anything I thought was ridiculous and do the part the way I knew to do it. I was getting more than a taste of what was ahead. There were things he could teach me, but I didn't think *these* things.

Our first session was really uncomfortable. Both of us came to it full of bad feelings and ready for battle—Bob furious that he hadn't got his way, and I was pissed that even after having proven myself, that meant nothing to him. A bad situation, and one that didn't seem likely to improve. We both left the rehearsal just as we had started it, if not worse. This was going to be some party.

The next time Bob and I saw each other was in Germany, on the first day of rehearsal at Bavaria Studios, twenty minutes outside Munich, where we shot all the Kit Kat Klub scenes. Despite the change in surroundings, things were still chilly between us.

When I arrived, Bob was already trying out some ideas with his choreographic assistants, Kathryn Doby and John Sharpe. Barely acknowledging me, Bob told Fred Werner, the rehearsal pianist, to play a specific section of "Two Ladies." Watching Bob go through some of the steps with the two German dancers, I couldn't help noticing the pleasure he took in performing. He was very good. Bob had gone to Hollywood to be a star. Despite his ambitions and smooth charm, it wasn't to be. After several movies, he transitioned to choreography and directing. I always wondered if, even unconsciously, he would have liked to play the part of the Emcee himself. Could his line "It's either Joel Grey or me" be taken that way? Performers don't ever stop thinking about performing somewhere in the back of their mind, especially if they are good, and Bob was really good. Plus he was a control freak, and the ultimate control over a part is to play it oneself.

I'll admit that I arrived in Germany with a chip on my shoulder; I was suspicious of anyone who wanted to change a hair of *Cabaret*. I had a lot riding on this. Since *George M!*, which had taken up a few years between its Broadway run and the national tour, I had done a couple of guest appearances on television. But this was a once-in-a-lifetime opportunity to re-create what I had done on Broadway in a major movie. It felt like I was the keeper of the flame from *Cabaret*'s original team. I couldn't let Bob "Fosse" it up.

As in our rehearsal back in New York, Bob created moves that were extremely mannered ("Five, six, seven, eight! No spontaneity please!"). I didn't think that suited the Kit Kat Klub. *My* Kit Kat Klub.

As we struggled with the undercurrent, the rehearsal turned into a kind of dare between Bob and me. He dug in harder with his specificity, while I continued to resist him, until it escalated into Bob's most unreasonable idea.

"Can you do a backflip?" he asked me.

"I don't think so," I replied.

"There's nothing to it. Let me show you. John, come over here," he said to his assistant. "I'll show you how this works. John, spot me."

We all watched as Bob threw himself up backward into the air, but he didn't make it. Instead, he came crashing to the ground and landed on his face. For several horrifyingly long seconds he lay there without moving. All of us around him were frozen with shock. Had he broken his neck? After a stunned moment, we all went to his aid. Bob stood up slowly, and with an arm around each assistant, he was taken to the studio infirmary.

When Bob came to the studio the next day, he had the usual cigarette hanging out of his mouth, but the whole left side of his face was black and blue. No one mentioned his injuries—or the backflip—again.

Even though the rehearsals were exceptionally long and exacting, they were exciting, too. Bob and I watched each other like hawks, but we definitely influenced each other's plans and ideas. We quietly rose to the challenge of realizing that this thing was not going to succeed without the combination of both strong opinions living in the space we had reluctantly come to share.

For rehearsal, Bob often required temporary set pieces so he could see how the numbers were going to look. The decor and lighting for the Kit Kat Klub were directly inspired by the work of George Grosz and Otto Dix, two artists who painted pessimistically realistic images of Weimar society and war. The club set, on its own soundstage, was always thick with smoke, which gave the scenes a great look but also made people sick. There was lots of coughing, and no one coughed more than Bob, who, having recovered from his fall, immediately proceeded to come down with a bad cold that led to a respiratory infection, which dogged him the whole time we were filming. Still, I don't recall having ever seen him without that dangling cigarette.

More than once we rehearsed a single routine for days only to have Bob throw it out, unsatisfied, and once more begin, "Five, six, seven, eight!" The "Money" number was probably the most complicated. He staged it two or three ways before he was satisfied.

"Hands, feet."

"Look at Liza."

"Look straight ahead."

"Look to the right, exactly after Liza."

"Remember, hands!"

For rehearsal, he wanted us in costume—not the real ones, which were being built, but a temporary long dress for Liza and a tailcoat, pants, top hat, and cane for me. This tailcoat came from "stock" costumes that were used for extras through the years. The pieces were cleaned after each actor used them, but the warmth of my body seemed to activate the old sweat. Let's say it was an olfactory explosion.

"It's like dancing with fifteen old Germans," Liza said with a shriek. Then I shrieked. Then we both shrieked.

I adored her. From the beginning, it was a we're-in-this-together relationship. I had known Liza before we arrived in Germany, but just as with Bob, only tangentially. I was bowled over when I saw her perform in a nightclub act at the Coconut Grove and on Broadway in *Flora the Red Menace*. And we would see each other socially from time to time, never failing to find something to laugh at.

Now, however, we were spending practically all day working and every night letting go. Each day started with an early-morning drive to the set from our hotel—the Residenz in Munich, where all the Americans were put up. My morning started a little earlier than Liza's. I waited in the lobby for her since she always seemed to need a little more time. Her faithful secretary, Deanna Wemble, would ring me in the lobby to say, "Liza will be right down." The cheerful English assistant, who rarely left the star's side, was the messenger of all "Minnelli stuff."

I understood Deanna's instinct to protect Liza. Yes, it was her job, but there was something about Liza that invited you to take care of her. I relished our morning rides to the studio, during which she would often fall asleep on my shoulder. I would have been upset to disturb her even on the morning that the drab backdrop of Munich's outskirts was transformed by Cat Stevens's brand-new song "Morning Has Broken" playing on a German radio station. The song always reminds me of our odyssey and closeness. When we neared the studio, I would give her a whisper, as you would a child.

Liza retained an air of vulnerability despite the fact that her parents were the great Judy Garland and the renowned director Vincente Minnelli, and that she had been performing professionally since the age of seventeen. By the time we found ourselves in Germany, her first marriage, to Peter Allen, had ended, even though they didn't officially divorce until years later.

We talked about her early life in Hollywood and my obsession with the theater over beer, schnapps, and dinner, which we shared most every night. (We often went to an Italian restaurant that Mussolini had apparently frequented; the food was great, even if the history was awful.) But we didn't have much energy to spend on anything other than the film we were making.

I totally admired Bob's relentless attention to detail and had just as high a bar for my own performance. I worked with a gifted dialogue coach, Osman Ragheb, so that my accent and dialect would be not just German but Berlinish, which turned out to be very specific (not unlike a Brooklyn accent vs. a Midwestern one). I had always loved languages, and Osman's coaching was so precise that I was even able to convince the German extras who had been hired to play the denizens of the Kit Kat Klub that I was a German actor.

From the outset, the German crew was leery that we were making a film that would continue to demonize their generation by holding them responsible for the sins of their fathers. The atmosphere at the studio was tense on both sides. At the end of the first week, one night after the last shot, the producers sent beer to the German crew as a gesture. Getting a bit drunk, as crews can, they all started spontaneously to sing a beer-hall song in the style of "Deutschland über Alles." It was upsetting and brought to mind the beer-garden scene from the show in which German youth lead the charge in singing "Tomorrow Belongs to Me."

When shooting the audience members in the Kit Kat Klub, it was important that the extras playing them be actually relaxed and having a good time so that their expressions would be authentic. One day before a take, I asked assistant director Wolfgang Glattes to give me a Berlin expression that would crack them up. I tried it out with my studied accent, and it worked like a charm. From that day on, they never doubted my veracity: "Of course, he's German. He's so funny." And therefore when the Emcee was entertaining the patrons of the Kit Kat Klub, the extras playing them were truly laughing. Amazingly enough, they took me, Mickey Katz's son from Cleveland, as one of their own.

For me the turning point in making *Cabaret* into a film came when, after six weeks of rehearsing, prerecording the numbers, and fine-tuning them once more, we actually started shooting. At that time, everyone involved went to the dailies to see on-screen what we had rehearsed for weeks, and it looked amazing, like nothing any of us had ever seen. Whatever it is that makes magic was doing its job brilliantly. It was all there: cinematographer Geoffrey Unsworth's perfect light-ing; authentic, compelling performances by Liza, me, and the Kit Kat Girls; and, of course, Bob's genius and vision. From that moment on, I had only the deepest respect for him as an artist. The struggle had been worth it. More than worth it.

Even though there always remained some reserve between us, Bob and I began to let down our guard. Having grown up in the world of burlesque and vaudeville (one of six children born to a vaudevillian father, Bob was a regular in his hometown Chicago's burlesque scene by the time he was in high school). He knew his way around sleaze and appreciated the blending of the outrageous and the sinister that I brought to the Emcee. He nicknamed me Mr. Porno. I knew he was pleased with a take when I saw a tiny smile on his face. That was like Fosse fireworks, an Oscar from Bobby.

Bob opened up somewhat to my ideas, but he was still pretty control-ling whenever I tried to change even a single element of his direction: *No variations, please!* That lasted until the very last scene we shot. It was one with two women mud-wrestling on the stage of the Kit Kat Klub, and it seemed to take forever. As if it weren't degrading enough for the two zaftig actresses to be down and dirty, they were also bleeding, because of sharp stones mistakenly left in the mud. We had already done many takes, shooting way past midnight, when Bob announced that we would do "just one more" before wrapping for the night. We were so exhausted that we didn't know if we had one more take in us. At the very end of the last take, I, as the Emcee and the wrestling match's gleeful referee, bent down, put some mud on my right forefinger, and smeared it across my upper lip. There was no particular button to this scene or indication for me to make the Hitler mustache and then give the "Heil Hitler" salute; it just popped into my head, so I did it. Bob screamed, "Cut!" Walking toward me in a rage, he asked, "Why did you do that?"

"That's how I work," I said calmly. "In that moment it felt like what I, as the Emcee, would do."

He walked off furious, and Wolfgang shouted, "That's a wrap!"

I was just glad to be done.

The next day, when the cast, crew, and extras were gathered to say goodbye, Wolfgang made a special announcement, bidding "alles sagen auf Wiedersehen," which meant that everyone should say goodbye to the Emcee, "Herr Joel Grey, who leaves us tonight for his home in New York. He is an esteemed American actor, and we are so grateful he joined us for this film here in Munich." Big silence. What? I wasn't German? I wasn't one of them? Their sense of betrayal was palpable. They had come to accept me as one of their own, and their wonderful reactions for the camera as audience members had been rich, broad, and wholly authentic.

I felt guilty for having tricked them, but the extras weren't the only ones who wound up feeling betrayed. Many months later, Bob finished his cut of *Cabaret* and showed it for the first time. I was excited and of course nervous as the lights went down in the anonymous LA screening room, because the footage I had seen from the dailies in Munich was so good. Geoffrey, who had done amazing cinematography on *Barry Lyndon*, was one of my favorite people involved with the film. He was a quiet, classy, good-looking man, and I could talk to him about anything. His vision was unique, and the small pieces of the musical numbers we filmed in Munich that I had seen were incredible.

So when in that screening room I watched all the work I had done cut into a million pieces, I was stunned to the point of tears. In Bob's first cut of the film, he used only snippets of the musical numbers. He had reduced the numbers to "ins and outs" so that they acted only as transitions or the glue between scenes. Not a single one was anywhere close to complete. That had to be one of the worst moments of my career.

What happened? Why? Perhaps it was total paranoia that was maybe connected to the idea that Liza should be the only star of the movie, which led Bob to make his first cut with only dribs and drabs of the Emcee's numbers. Maybe he thought they distracted from her. There was also the possibility that Bob made the book scenes more important because of his desire to become a nonmusical director (which he brilliantly went on to do with *Lenny*, the Lenny Bruce biopic starring Dustin Hoffman) and *Star Eighty*.

I couldn't believe that my work in the film had been decimated. I walked out of the screening room without saying a word to Bob, and then I went crazy in a nearby phone booth.

"Marty, I can't believe what I just saw," I said over the phone to one of the film's producers. "There's not one complete number. Not one number with a beginning, middle, and end. I'm just connective tissue!"

"Relax," he said. "I know what you're talking about. I saw it last night. Trust me. The numbers *will* be there—intact."

Still, a few weeks later, when Jo and I and all the cast, studio heads, producers, and Bob flew up to San Francisco to see a sneak preview of the movie, I *was* worried.

The Northpoint Theatre had already filled with people for this unadvertised preview when we snuck in and hid in the back row. From the minute the film began, it was pure magic. All my fears vanished as the full version of "Willkommen" ended to an ovation—in a movie theater.

It all worked. Liza's comic timing was unreal, her singing thrilling, and at the end of the film she truly broke your heart. The numbers were phenomenal, but the one that meant the most to me, just as it had on Broadway, was "If You Could See Her," because it was the most overtly anti-Semitic. Being Jewish, I felt it was vital that we show those anti-Semites for what they were. Well, watching the scene on the big screen, it was more than ugly. It was hideous and just right. The line "She wouldn't look Jewish . . ." came down like a nail on a coffin.

The audience in the San Francisco theater went crazy. We knew it was going to be something big, but just how big took all of us by surprise. *Cabaret* was not only an immediate success at the box office after its release, on February 13, 1972, but it also was winning many industry awards, such as a Golden Globe for Best Motion Picture–Comedy or Musical. The biggest deal, however, was the film's ten Academy Award nominations, including one for me as Best Supporting Actor.

March 27, 1973, the day of the 45th Academy Awards, was one of the hottest spring days on record. But truth be told, it could have been snowing and I wouldn't have noticed. I was freaked out. Even though I had been nominated for an Oscar, I was all but sure I wouldn't win. My parents, on the other hand, were already working on *their* acceptance speeches for friends, family, and the press. That's how convinced they were that I'd take home the statue. My dad, now in his early sixties, never wavered from being my biggest fan. At home in LA, they dedicated an entire wall to my achievements with framed photos, newspaper clips, and a full-sized poster of . . . me, leading Dad to his joke that "the apartment is decorated in early Joel Grey." My mother, meanwhile, gave an interview to *The Los Angeles Times*, which reported that I didn't go into show business: "Says his mother, 'I pushed him.' "

The Katz vote aside, Al Pacino was the clear front-runner for his role as Michael Corleone in *The Godfather*. Even if his performance hadn't been perfection, which it was, musical movies just didn't have the respect that serious dramas did. Yes, of course I was thrilled to be nominated. But it's pretty much a fact that everyone really wants to win.

Larry Hagman, my next-door neighbor in the Malibu Colony and one of my most cherished friends for years, stopped by for coffee. I'm sure he sensed my tension, because he decided to take me out to get a haircut, lunch, anything to distract me. He did a pretty good job, too.

Larry was always trying to loosen me up. While I was careful and alert, Larry was a wild man. His mother had been Mary Martin, who had left her son in the care of his grandmother when he was just seven years old. After she married Richard Halliday a couple of years later, Larry was shipped off to military school and eventually became estranged from her. I have no idea how Larry turned into such a sweet man. Other than his sixty-year marriage to his beloved Maj, there was nothing conventional about him. A card-carrying member of the Peace and Freedom Party, he thought nothing of wearing quirky costumes while walking down the beach or requesting a joke in exchange when asked for his autograph. And he loved to smoke pot. Once, while we were soaking in his Jacuzzi, where he particularly liked to get high, he insisted on my taking a puff. I, the guy who got drunk off one grasshopper. You don't get much squarer than that. But I tried it. (It just made me dizzy.) Larry didn't seem to have many fears, and I loved that in him.

Larry got me back home just in time for me to put on my tuxedo and be ready by three in the afternoon. That's when Jo, looking spectacular in Halston, and I got into the waiting limousine and were waved off ceremoniously by my big buddy and Maj, the sun and sand blazing all around.

I felt like a star when Carol Burnett, a pal and the host for the Oscars that night, mentioned me in her opening monologue: "I knew him when he was Joel Katz . . ." And she did! But it was hard to keep smiling as the tension mounted. Best Supporting Actor, thank God, is one of the earlier awards given, so at least I didn't have to wait long.

The award's presenters, Diana Ross and James Coburn, opened the envelope and the singer, in her signature breathy voice, said, "And the winner's Joel Grey."

I was out of my body as I kissed Jo and ran up onstage. I can't recall my exact words because the moment was such a blur. All I remember is starting with, "Don't let anyone tell you this isn't a great thrill." But that didn't begin to convey how I felt. As one of only eight people to win both the Tony and Academy Award for the same role, I was in amazing company that included Yul Brynner for *The King and I*, Anne Bancroft for *The Miracle Worker*, and Rex Harrison for *My Fair Lady*. The actors who made the difficult transition from stage to screen were quite a group, and I was grateful to be a part of it.

The rest of the night was as much of a blur as my acceptance speech. At the Governors Ball, Liza, who won for Best Actress, and I were giddy. Bob, who took home the Best Director award, and I exchanged more muted congratulations for *Cabaret*, which won for cinematography, art direction, sound, film editing, and music. We were pretty much back to square one in our relationship, but nothing could keep me from feeling good.

More clearly etched into my mind is the limo ride back to Malibu, during which Jo and I talked about little things.

"Did you like the quiche?" I asked in the dark, holding hands with my beautiful wife, and looking out onto the Pacific Coast Highway under the moonlight.

"I thought it was an odd choice," she said.

"You looked so beautiful in your dress. The photographers were falling all over themselves to take your picture."

"Well, I am the Best Supporting Actor's wife."

I didn't think I could feel any happier, but I was wrong. When the limousine dropped us at home, standing in front of our door was this enormous trophy that Larry had left for me, just in case I came home empty-handed. I picked it up and read the words he had engraved on it: TO JOEL GREY, THE BEST FUCKING NEIGHBOR AWARD.

"You'll see. This time will be different," Liza said, "and we'll be together."

CHAPTER THIRTEEN

Opening the shutters of the Gritti and looking out onto the water, I saw a boat delivery of fresh bread, which made me call room service immediately.

Jo and I, both of us so happy to wake up in a beautiful room in the fifteenth-century Venetian palazzo turned hotel, luxuriating in our bed with linen sheets, laughing, loving, and enjoying each other—my wish coming true.

A knock at the door interrupted. "Buongiorno!" said the waiter, setting the tray upon the bed before giving a quick bow and leaving. The two of us were giddy with steamed milk, strong coffee, and fresh baked pastries *con marmellata*. How far I had come since my last time in Italy, at nineteen. I slept upon a straw mattress in a simple pensione in Positano!

When I was growing up, no one in my family had ever been abroad. What had once been relegated to movie screens, art museums, books, and personal fantasies was finally in the realm of possibility because of the international success of *Cabaret*. The financial perks it brought us allowed Jo and me to pursue beauty in new places. The joyous period in my relationship with Jo that began with *Cabaret* only improved after winning an Oscar. And because Jo had given up her career to support mine, we shared my achievements, which only made them richer.

We both loved to travel, and now during our first trip to Venice, there was not an instant that was less than perfect. The moment we set foot on the vaporetto from the airplane into town, we were overwhelmed. As if it were our honeymoon, we did everything, getting totally lost in the city's mazelike magic. We were corny American tourists, taking pictures with the pigeons of Piazza San Marco, sloshing in the high tides, visiting the Jewish ghetto on Giudecca, and hopping a small boat to the island of Torcello for a lunch of vitello tonnato and wine in a garden. Our friends Regina Resnik (the opera singer who was in the 1987 revival of *Cabaret*) and her husband, Arbit Blatas, a well-known painter, showed us around the city, which they made their part-time home. And one night in the lobby of the Gritti, we ran into Truman Capote, whom I knew through our mutual lawyer, Alan Schwartz, and off all of us went to dinner at Harry's Bar.

Just being alone with my wife, however, tumbling into our four-poster bed at the hotel for a nap after hours of walking, was more than enough. With the kids back in New York with Nellie, we became acutely aware of the fact that we were getting to do so much of what we had dreamed and talked about.

That year, it also seemed like a good idea to move from the second-floor rear apartment on 87th Street and Central Park West to a spacious eleventh-floor apartment at 1120 Fifth Avenue that overlooked Central Park's reservoir. Although we now lived in an old-money Upper East Side building, we simplified substantially. We focused less on furnishings, which made for a great, neutral background for our small but growing art collection filled with works by friends such as Jim Dine and R. B. Kitaj. Hiring John Saladino was the last right touch. The interior designer built platforms on which were placed mattresses slip-covered in duck all along the front windows that looked out onto the reservoir.

The whole place was not unlike our Malibu beach house. We loved living on the ocean, thriving in the sensibility of light and sky and water. The New York apartment had a clean look, like our tiny cottage in LA with its bleached floors and sun-drenched patio. Frank Israel—the LA–based architect revered for his innovations to the contemporary Southern California style made famous by Frank Gehry—had recently redesigned the house after an awful fire during which no one was home or hurt. It seemed that on both coasts, simple was good.

Jimmy and Jen were loving being back in New York. They went to great schools, and on the weekends we took family trips out to Westhampton or Nantucket with a close group of pals. James was always marching to the beat of his own drum, doing boy things such as building model cars and dropping water balloons from our apartment window on people walking along Fifth. Jennifer's idea of fun was more sophisticated. She was an independent teenager who sometimes did things I thought were inappropriate. Teenagers hate that word, which Jennifer let me know in no uncertain terms. (Hmm . . . kindred spirits!)

I never stopped worrying about both of my children. From the moment Jennifer and James were born, we were very present in both of their lives. I would go to PTA meetings, pick the kids up from school, and take them to their lessons, which my flexible schedule often allowed. I loved doing all of it, because it made me feel complete and like a good father. So I was always close to both my kids.

Winning the Academy Award meant that many more varied projects came my way that allowed me to work steadily. One job offer I didn't think I wanted to do, however, was tour the US with Liza. Capitalizing on our success in *Cabaret* with a nightclub act was something of a no-brainer. But I hadn't forgotten how I'd loathed working in nightclubs, the people eating, drinking, and smoking during the show. "You'll see. This time will be different," Liza said, "and we'll be together."

It was always hard to say no to Liza; her enthusiasm was infectious.

Of course, she turned out to be absolutely right. From our very first show at the Riviera in Las Vegas, we were the talk of the town. Fred Ebb, who had already been writing Liza's act, wrote one for me. Ron Lewis staged it with a large steamer trunk. The beautiful prop, covered in stickers from all the places I had ever played (and some I hadn't), magically opened up, and I climbed on top to sing a big *George M!* medley. I even tap-danced on top of it. I opened the show, then Liza did her dynamite act, and then I joined her to do a couple of encores such as "The Money Song." There was never an empty table or seat, even in the vast arenas we sometimes played. Liza, loose, savvy, generous, and often hilarious, was a great onstage partner.

One night on the tour, the stage manager in the theater gave her the cue to introduce me before I was ready. The show had been arranged so that I went on first, with the orchestra playing my overture, followed by a drum roll, then Liza's announcing from a backstage mic, "Ladies and gentlemen, my friend, Joel Grey." That night, however, when she said my name, I still wasn't dressed. More specifically, I didn't have any pants on. I came out onstage anyway—in pleated shirt, bow tie, black kneesocks, and shoes. The audience, which loves it when something goes awry, screamed.

I went back offstage, and my overture started over. Again Liza announced, "Ladies and gentlemen, Joel Grey." This time, however, I came out fully dressed to start the show. Never one to be outdone, when it was time for Liza to make her entrance and I announced, "Ladies and gentlemen, my friend, Liza Minnelli," she came out in curlers and a robe. The audience was screaming again when she added, "*I'll* be right back."

The Oscar led to more interesting screen roles. The director Robert Altman offered me a part in his revisionist Western *Buffalo Bill and the Indians*. As Nate Salisbury, Buffalo Bill's press agent, I got to act with Burt Lancaster, Harvey Keitel, Shelley Duvall, Geraldine Chaplin, and Paul Newman, a fellow Clevelander, who starred as Buffalo Bill. Bob Altman's sets were very informal, creative, and family-oriented, so

Jo and the kids visited me in Calgary where we spent three months shooting a complete re-creation of "Buffalo Bill's Wild West" show.

That same year, I was cast as a creepy denizen and mysterious presence of the Viennese demimonde in *The Seven-Per-Cent Solution*, directed by Herbert Ross, a friend with whom I'd worked on an ABC TV pilot in the sixties. In the film, I played Lowenstein, a suspicious character who pops up all over Vienna. Again I found myself in another great group of actors, including Alan Arkin, Robert Duvall, Lawrence Olivier, and Vanessa Redgrave.

Despite these amazing experiences, the thought of abandoning Broadway for Hollywood never crossed my mind. The theater always suited my soul. I went back to Broadway in 1975 (once again at the Palace Theatre) in *Goodtime Charley*, an unlikely musical about Joan of Arc and the Dauphin Charles VII of France, aka Charley. The score, by Larry Grossman and Hal Hackady, was unequivocally good and made all the better by the stunning orchestrations of Jonathan Tunick, *the* Broadway orchestrator of his generation. I loved the piece—and in particular my character. His evolution over the course of the musical from a dolt to a great king was due to the belief that Joan of Arc (played by Ann Reinking) had in him.

When *Goodtime Charley* opened on Broadway, I received my usual break-a-leg telegrams from friends—this time including one from Bob Fosse, Ann's boyfriend at the time, who wrote, "Even when you do the steps backwards you are terrific." He wasn't the only one from my *Cabaret* family who wired. Kander and Ebb sent one that read: "Dear Joel, Long live the King! Love, John and Fred."

Unfortunately, the show got mixed reviews. The critics warmly embraced Ann's and my work, and they loved Rouben Ter-Arutunian's sets and Willa Kim's costumes. But they were hard on the book and score. Fortunately *Goodtime Charley* had enough going for it that we didn't end up on Joe Allen's wall of shame (the wall of the restaurant displaying show cards of all the productions that are notorious flops). In fact the producers didn't close *Goodtime Charley* until almost four months later when I had to leave the show to shoot *Buffalo Bill* with Bob Altman.

In the years right after *Cabaret* I felt much more secure not only in my career but also in my life with Jo. A sweet time continued for us; we enjoyed our good fortune, our kids, and each other more than ever. But just as my work began to have its ups and downs, so did my marriage. Although Jo and I had our volatile side, our fights were so frustrating because they were always the same. We would have a disagreement about an emotional issue, and when I would bring it up days or weeks later, Jo more often than not had no idea what I was talking about. "I just don't remember what happened and you are so definite," she would say to me. I accused her of forgetting as a way to close herself off and once again became a bully.

We needed someone with authority to help us move the communication forward, perhaps even teach us *how* to fight. So around 1980, we began seeing a couples therapist on West End Avenue. What I realized during those sessions was that we didn't really know each other when we got married and had a lot of catching up to do. Jo felt pushed around and not heard, which were the last things I wanted her to feel. Through our work with the therapist, I felt that Jo and I had come to a new, better place in our relationship. More than the superficial pleasures we enjoyed from my success in the theater, we were getting to the deep issues that would form a solid bond. Together we were arriving at such a place of intimacy that I couldn't imagine being happier or more contented with my life. Truly, I was no longer alone.

Encouraged by our therapist, I thought it was time to tell Jo about my past. I had reached a place of such rightness and trust with my wife that I wanted to reveal all of myself to her. Authenticity became an imperative.

It was late in the afternoon—the light was beautiful coming into the bedroom from a window that faced east—and we were sitting on the bed when I said to her, "Honey, I need to talk to you about something."

Of course I was nervous; this was a precarious declaration, one that I had worked hard to keep hidden from everyone, including myself. But I knew the time was right.

"There's something I've wanted to tell you for a long, long time. But I never did because I wasn't secure enough in myself, in us. Until now.

"There's no easy way to say this so I am just going to come right out with it. When we first met I had struggled for years with feelings I had . . . for men."

As soon as I made the declaration, a flood of words followed as if they had been dammed up by the idea that I had kept undisclosed for so long.

"It really tore me apart. But, Jo, when I met you everything changed. *Everything.* I was so taken and immediately crazy in love with you. Those other thoughts I once had were no longer important. And loving you all this time has made me know that this is where I always wanted to be. I love you so much, and I don't want there ever to be any dishonesty between us."

I had revealed my dark secret and was happy. Who knew how keeping all that inside had affected our marriage? Now we could move on with compassion, love, authenticity . . . But as I sat there waiting for a response, searching her face for a reaction, any reaction, my elation quickly turned to dread.

I had assumed she would understand my admission as the closing of the door on my past. In my scenario, she would throw her arms around me and say, "I'm so grateful you've shared this with me. I love you so much, too." But she didn't say that. When I reached out to embrace her, it was clear she had gone away.

As the days went by in slow motion, I hoped that she'd come to me after she had time to process what I had told her. But she never did. We never spoke about it again, and Jo became increasingly impatient, standoffish, and unreachable.

The change in our relationship made me realize that I had greatly misjudged who she was and where she was in her life. I started to wonder if our happiness, our closeness was something I had imagined. For so many years, I knew the revelation of my complex sexuality wasn't easy to take in. Still, I couldn't help thinking that she had been looking for some reason to distance herself, and that perhaps she was already on her way out.

I decided that talking about my past had been a mistake and didn't bring it up again. If she brought it up, maybe then we could talk about it again. But for now, we spoke of other things. We also came to the conclusion that there wasn't any reason to continue therapy together.

We had been through perhaps more than our fair share of upsets and challenges, but after a bit things always righted themselves—or so I thought. As our marriage hobbled along, I searched for a way to fix this latest upset. I understood from our therapy sessions that she had never forgiven me for not supporting her talent and career. After I made her give up her job in the Broadway musical *She Loves Me* to join me while I was touring with *Stop the World,* Jo hadn't really worked again. So I proposed that she and I might work together to produce films. I wanted to make it up to her.

Jo had always been astute about the theater, art, and films—always an incisive reader of material. One night, out to dinner with the *Mommie Dearest* producer and Paramount president Frank Yablans, we casually mentioned a project that we had long been discussing, about father-and-son performers in the Catskills. Frank, who was at 20th Century Fox, loved the idea and wanted to set Jo up with an office at his studio where as a producer she could find the right writer for this project. In a matter of days, there was an office with her name on it at Fox, where, as a talented producer to be reckoned with, she felt validated.

Not long afterward, we also began developing a TV movie at CBS about Harvey Milk, the first openly gay person voted into public office. Looking back, the subject matter was a sublimation of the conversation Jo and I couldn't have. But we chalked it up to political beliefs; the issue of gay rights felt natural and important to both of us. Jo and

I dove into researching the biopic, interviewing Milk's associates and reading about his background. Our passion for the subject was apparent, and we made it to the final approval stage. That, however, was when it was dropped without explanation. Word was that someone high up at the network decided that TV wasn't ready for the Harvey Milk story.

After the project was killed, I started to question our motives in wanting to make a movie about a gay man. Were we distancing ourselves from the information I had told her in our bedroom that afternoon, or trying to find a way to bring up the conversation? In fact I questioned my motives in having told her about my feelings for men in the first place. What had been in it for me? My life—work, our family—was everything I had hoped for. So why did I choose this moment to push the issue? And what happened afterward makes my motive for having told her—that I wanted to bring us closer—even more suspect.

The growing anger and distance between us created a void that eventually compelled me to turn to friends for comfort. I began spending time with two old friends, both gay men, married to women with kids, who through the years still had the occasional encounter with other men. Confused and lonely, I was searching for closeness and connection.

This wasn't the first time. A handful of times over the course of our twenty-four years together, I lied to myself and her. Whenever I was exceptionally lonely at home, I sought out men, often in the same boat, most of them married. Years could go by in between these encounters.

I told myself this wasn't being unfaithful. As I saw it, if I had slept with other women, which I knew was possible, *that* would have been cheating. My intimate male friendships were always with guys who had made the same choice as I in adapting their needs. None of us wanted to throw lives and families into chaos by leaving our wives. No, we would have our time together—and then go quickly home.

But if I had been honest, I would have asked myself what these times with men truly meant. The closest answer I could come up with was that it was about taking care of oneself, the self that existed before there was a wife, the self that I never stopped struggling with. I never looked for what was missing in another woman. I needed the safe haven of men.

Yet I couldn't imagine my life without Jo and the kids. I loved her more than I had ever loved anyone else. She felt differently. Shortly after James went off to college in 1981, not long after our twenty-fourth wedding anniversary, Jo told me that she was leaving, and just like that she moved out of our home and never came back.

"These are not invisible men."

CHAPTER FOURTEEN

Right in the middle of my show's second number, Randy Newman's "Short People," which I sang standing on stilts made of tin cans, the sound system went dead. In that moment, I was suddenly faced with an amphitheater of 7,500 staring ticketholders. That kind of silence on stage is unforgettable.

I was depressed before I even stepped onto the vast stage of the Garden State Arts Center, in New Jersey. But having made a commitment to play this date after thinking, back in LA, that it might take my mind off the pain of Jo's leaving, I had to go through with it. However, the morning of the show, she called to tell me that Minnie, one of our two beloved Abyssinian cats, had got out of the house in Brentwood, where Jo now lived permanently. She had found the cat's dead body on the patio, a victim of a coyote attack. I was furious at her for having allowed Minnie out of the house, for leaving, for the whole crappy thing.

And now the sound was out in the massive outdoor theater.

Having been taught as an actor that ad-libbing was unacceptable, I never got good at it. I said something politely, and the sound came on, and the show continued. After a few more numbers, the sound failed again. Then it went back on, then failed again—and something in me exploded.

"If you can't get this thing working," I said holding my microphone out in front of me like an assault weapon and looking directly at the sound booth, "then you can stick it up your ass."

Whoa! There was a collective gasp from 7,500 now-stunned people. As I realized what I had just said, I silently prayed for the stage to open up and swallow me. Mickey Katz's pride and joy, his firstborn, and the Cleveland Play House's favorite son had not been raised to lose it onstage. I couldn't imagine ever being forgiven for such a lewd lapse and utter loss of control. After the show ended, I sped offstage toward my dressing room, not even considering taking a bow, when the stage manager came after me, yelling, "Get back out there!" When I did, I found 7,500 people standing and applauding wildly. I guess the audience understood that I was human even if I couldn't understand that myself.

I desperately hoped that Jo would change her mind and come back to me, although everyone kept telling me to forget her. Not even the wise and forceful Grandma Fanny, who had spent a lifetime getting people to do what she wanted, could persuade her otherwise. After Jo had gone to visit my ninety-three-year-old grandmother to tell her side of the story, Fanny called me. "It's no good, *Mein Kind*," Fanny said. "She's jealous of you."

My grandma turned out to be right. Jo was jealous of my career and my certainty. But she was also angry that I had kept her from having a career of her own. However, it was my past with men that she could not forgive. Not only did she refuse to return to me but she also refused to come back to New York. Right after we sold our apartment at 1120 Fifth Avenue, she wanted nothing to do with sorting out the "stuff" of our twenty-four years together. "You do it," she said. I went through hundreds of photos of all of us in happier times. Pictures of our wedding, the children as babies, trips—Jo didn't want any of it. Adamantly focused on the future, she was not going to look back.

I moved into a sublet, a third-floor walk-up on West 11th Street where I immediately got sick with a terrible flu, as if everything, even my immune system, had given up. I felt abandoned, rudderless, and totally without value. My whole life was coming undone. I had done everything in my power *not* to be homosexual, no matter the cost, and now the whole construct was falling apart around me. The destruction had such far-reaching effects, just as I had feared. Although they were already young adults who had moved out of the house, Jennifer and James distanced themselves from me. I never had a direct conversation with either of them about my sexuality, but I knew that Jo had to have told them everything.

I didn't know if the kids were angry with me. So many people we knew, including parents of Jennifer's and James's friends, were divorced. Jo and I had created such a strong picture together; we were the couple that had made it. None of our friends could believe it when we split. Hell, I couldn't believe it.

I wept all the time. I lost my taste for food and forgot to sleep. I watched television every night in some kind of trance, waiting patiently for snow to appear on the screen. I recorded an insane message for my answering machine in Yiddish. I had too much time on my hands. A good friend decided I needed a cat. I didn't think she was right—look how much good a puppy did Jo and me in the end. But my friend was right. The cat's name was Betty, and she was a godsend who ended up traveling with me when I went on tour for months.

The end of my marriage was like any other loss in that acceptance didn't come all at once but in slow and painful stages: Jo's moving out; Jo's not coming back; and then a divorce process that further depressed me in its expense and ugliness. By the time we were officially divorced, in 1982, I was utterly worn out and mistrustful not only of others but also of my own instincts.

The fact that I was free to see who I wanted to see was for me never a cause for celebration. I had never wanted to be free. Ever since I was a little boy I wanted to be part of a loving family of my own creation, and I grew up in a time when recognized unions and children were unthinkable for gay men—unless, of course, they were married to women. But if the idea of being openly gay seemed difficult then, at this particular time, when an unnamed and terrifying disease was killing gay men everywhere, it seemed unimaginable.

The first person I knew to get sick with this mystery illness was Kris, a trainer at my gym. I asked some other member what happened to him when I hadn't seen him for weeks.

"I heard he's very sick," the gym member said.

"What do you mean?"

"You know. He's got *it*."

He didn't have to say more. "It" was enough to know I would probably never see Kris again—and to question the contact I had with him in the past. Had I used equipment after him? Did we hug each other goodbye? Stupid things felt scary.

And no gay man was safe. The bombshell that Rock Hudson had contracted the virus was tragic proof of that point. Having lived his life in the closet, the classic matinee idol's story had a heartbreaking end. When he became the first public figure to announce that he had AIDS, just ten weeks before his death, at the age of fifty-nine, in 1985, Rock was no longer the handsome leading man from *Giant* or *McMillan & Wife*. He was gaunt and suffered from Kaposi's sarcoma, the lesions that afflicted many with AIDS. As if the disease itself weren't cruel enough, homophobia added to the pain. Full of venom and judgment, loud voices said that Rock, a truly nice guy, deserved not only to suffer but also to die because of his sexual practices.

It was heartbreaking for me to reconcile the vibrant star—with whom I had spent some delightful time in Italy while shooting *Come September*—with the wasted man further ripped apart in the tabloids. It seemed as if overnight AIDS was attacking so many people who were important to me.

Ted, my early publicist, boyfriend, and friend, had in the intervening years become very powerful in Hollywood. When I heard he was sick, we hadn't been in touch. Still I knew that he never did get married, have a family, or come out. He remained one of those industry bachelors who people said never settled down because they were so busy with their careers.

My longtime stage manager, Rick, lost his young partner, David, while we were on tour together. In between shows at the Venetian Room at the Fairmont Hotel in San Francisco, Rick found me in my dressing room and said, "David died about an hour ago." He was only in his twenties.

The hardest of all for me, however, was Larry Kert, my great longtime friend. After *West Side Story*, Larry became the go-to guy, someone who could do anything in the theater. He and his longtime partner, Ron Pullen, had made a terrific life together, and Larry never lost his humor, even when I visited him late in his illness at their apartment on Horatio Street.

Ron opened the door, we hugged, and he took me to his lifetime lover, who, always so robust, was now emaciated. Still, Larry was trying to be his sweet self. "Hi, brother," I managed to say while bending down to embrace his disappearing body. We told each other we loved each other, and in his presence I wasn't afraid of all the rumors about this awful illness. I hugged and kissed him, not knowing how much longer I would have to do those things. After I left, though, I fell apart. I sat down on that stoop on Horatio Street and bawled. I was in LA when Larry died but flew back to be a part of the memorial service. Ron asked if I wanted to perform, and I did. I sang "Danny Boy," the song that played that time at the Belvedere Hotel. "Why 'Danny Boy'?" I imagined people asking. Nobody knew why, but I did.

I wanted to reenter life but wasn't sure what that meant. I never imagined that would mean living as a gay man. Having spent so many years pushing those feelings down, I didn't know how to "be gay." I needed practice, but AIDS served only to reinforce my caution.

My first job after the divorce, acting in and directing a summer-stock revival of *George M!*, turned out to be just the tonic I needed.

I was always a happy man working on a play or musical, and this was no exception. I knew the show well, enjoyed playing George Cohan, and loved directing it with an assist from my longtime friend Charlie Repole.

I've always felt that the intimacy of the theater, and trust necessary between actors, made for flirting, fantasizing about sex, and actually clicking with someone. Well that's exactly what happened. Paul was handsome, talented, and married. For me, it was just good to feel affection and passion. It seemed like forever since I had been pursued. After the show closed, a friend offered me his house on Nantucket, and for three days we enjoyed uninterrupted pleasure. We took walks on the beach, made dinner, made love, went to sleep, woke up, and made love again. I had never had that continuity of sleeping with a man and waking up with him in the morning. It was like being a whole human being.

For a few days, there were just the two of us in this world we created within the confines of a beautiful, old, beat-up beach house. We never left it. Neither of us thought it was wise to be seen in public together, so the closeness we felt for each other still had the element of hiding that had always been a part of my relationships with other men.

The idea that love and sex with a man was bound with humiliation and even the threat of death created a brutal contradiction that guys like me had to learn to live with. But as I sat in the audience of the Public Theater in July of 1985, watching Larry Kramer's *The Normal Heart*, all the outrage and sadness and shame that I had kept as confined as my sexuality came to the surface.

The play, which was already the talk of New York even though it was only in previews, was an unrelenting and unapologetic discussion of AIDS, a frightening subject most people did not want to deal with. From the moment I walked into the theater, I couldn't believe what I was looking at. The set, designed by Eugene Lee and Keith Raywood, had stark white walls covered with the names of people who had died from the disease. Too many names. I froze at the sight of names of friends I didn't know had succumbed.

Even though AIDS had been declared an epidemic by the Centers for Disease Control in 1981, because it was thought to be only a gay man's disease, little to nothing was being done to combat it. *The Normal Heart* blew the story open. Within moments of the start of the play, a patient walks out of a doctor's office and says, "I'm her twenty-eighth case, and sixteen of them are dead."

No one was talking like this at the time, and that was just the first of many shocking moments in the play. There were shocking lines, such as that of a doctor who calls AIDS "the most insidious killer I've ever seen or studied or heard about" and "Who cares if a faggot dies?" And there were OMG moments such as when the central character, Ned Weeks, Larry Kramer's autobiographical writer and gay activist, is kissed fully on the mouth by Felix, a reporter from the *New York Times*, who also is gay. Nothing quite like that had been seen in the theater.

The Normal Heart was devastating, frightening, and inspiring. I didn't know people who were activists in the way that Larry, or Ned, was. I didn't come from a world where gay men were out and loud and proud. My model had been the quietly refined bachelor such as Charlie Baker or the married man who snuck around, like me. Larry and the Gay Men's Health Crisis (GMHC), an AIDS service organization that he had helped found, were a relatively new phenomenon that inspired and frightened me. I had an immediate gut reaction. During intermission, I saw Larry and blurted out: "If there is ever a time for me to be in this play, know that I'll do anything to make that happen." It was chutzpah, but I needed to do this play, as an actor and probably as something else, too.

A few weeks later I got a call from Joe Papp, the Public Theater's founder and director. He wanted to know if I could take over the role of Ned Weeks. I could hardly believe what I was hearing. But it came with other disturbing information. Brad Davis, the actor who originated the role, had been diagnosed with AIDS. Davis, who rose to fame playing a drug smuggler imprisoned in Turkey in the film *Midnight Express* and kept his illness a secret for many years, had contracted the virus from intravenous drug use.

When I told a friend familiar with the play that I was taking over the part, he thought it might be smart for me to find out whether kissing someone with AIDS was dangerous, since playing Ned would mean kissing the man who played Felix. I didn't know anything about the actor or have any reason to believe he was ill. But this was the height of AIDS paranoia, when people wondered about contracting the virus through the air or by shaking someone's hand.

It was recommended that I contact Dr. Michael Gottlieb at UCLA, a leading AIDS researcher who also treated Rock Hudson. I asked him whether he thought there was any threat kissing a man about whom I had no previous knowledge. After a rather long silence, Dr. Gottlieb said, "Let me ask you something. Do you have to kiss him?"

"Yes, it's crucial to the play."

"Then I wouldn't do the play."

It was a tough conversation during a tough time, but it turned out to be nothing more than an academic exercise, because not even a leading researcher in the field was going to deter me from taking this role. I had spent so much of my life being ashamed of who I was that I somehow knew it would be freeing and therapeutic to inhabit a character completely unabashed about being gay. Maybe Ned could teach me something about self-acceptance.

My small act of disobedience brought me close to Ned, a role that turned out to be as transformative to play as I imagined. The character was just as powerful and outspoken as the man who created him. In the strength of his beliefs, Larry Kramer was a killer. While I had spent so much of my existence afraid of anyone finding out about certain feelings inside of me, Larry and Ned were the complete opposite. A real fighter, this character was out there shouting to the world that something had to be done because people were dying.

Ned has a long aria toward the end of the play that struck me to my core from the first time I heard it, and every night that I spoke it:

"I belong to a culture that includes Proust, Henry James, Tchaikovsky, Cole Porter, Plato, Socrates, Aristotle, Alexander the Great, Michelangelo, Leonardo da Vinci, Christopher Marlowe, Walt Whitman, Herman Melville, Tennessee Williams, Byron, E. M. Forster, Lorca, Auden, Francis Bacon, James Baldwin, Harry Stack Sullivan, John Maynard Keynes, Dag Hammarskjöld," Ned says. "These are not invisible men."

"The only way we'll have real pride," he says, "is when we demand recognition of a culture that isn't just sexual. It's all there, all through history we've been there, but we have to claim it, and identify who was in it, and articulate what's in our minds and hearts, and all our creative contributions to this Earth, and until we do that, until we organize ourselves by block, by neighborhood, by city, by state, into a united and visible community that fights back, we're doomed. That's how I want to be defined, as one of the men who fought the war."

Ned forced me to look at the parts of myself I had tried to hide for so long. Although no one knew it except me, saying those words to the audience was like revealing and standing up for myself in front of the world. Eight times a week, I got to be a gay man, a remarkable gay man, and every night that felt as full, as true, as passionate, and as authentic as I ever felt in my life.

My experience in *The Normal Heart* was just the beginning of a journey of self-discovery. But it was meaningful to me that the first moment I truly recognized a part of myself as homosexual didn't happen on an analyst's couch, during affairs with men, or after my divorce. It happened *onstage*.

The audience felt the transformative power of the play, too. During the last scene, in which Ned and Felix get married in the hospital just before Felix dies, we heard sobbing most every performance. So many were overcome with emotion. A minority, however, didn't care for the play, or more specifically, were offended by it. I learned early into the

show's run that some fans of my earlier, more mainstream and popular shows weren't quite ready to see me as an out, gay activist. One
night, when I stripped to my shorts in a hospital examination scene,
I became aware of a rustling in the third row, and then a little muffled
talking, like an argument. This was a small theater in which three-
quarters of the audience was really close. So when a man and woman
stood up, maneuvered down their row, and left, I could see them as
clearly as they saw me. It didn't bother me, though, when it happened
that night or on the many nights it happened thereafter. Instead I sensed
a kind of triumph that I was a part of a story told so well that it brought
on such strong reaction.

My children came from LA to see me in the play. Although I was
apprehensive, it meant a great deal to me for Jennifer and James to hear
me saying Ned's words as if they were mine. If regular audience members felt the power of watching me kiss a man passionately onstage,
how much more powerful was it for my daughter and son, who knew
that this was a part of their dad? I had carried around such guilt after
Jo and I split. It was all my fault that my family and my children's hearts
were broken. Yes, it was Jo who left. But I was the father and husband
who had been attracted to other men. There was no more shameful
position than that. So when after the play Jennifer and James greeted
me with tears in their eyes and loving, long hugs, I was relieved that
they had accepted what was nothing short of a declaration onstage.

Jennifer was able to relate to my work not just as my daughter but
also as an actress in her own right. Ever since I could remember, even
before she spent her Saturdays watching me from the wings in *Cabaret*,
Jennifer wanted to act. Although clearly the apple hadn't fallen far from
the tree, when Jennifer didn't want to go to college because she wanted
to be an actor, I worried. Knowing how hard it is to deal with this business, I was very protective—and negative about her acting full-time
right away.

She had already appeared in the films *Red Dawn* and *The Cotton Club*,
but it wasn't until I saw Jennifer in *American Flyers*, starring Kevin Cost-

ner, that I fully supported her decision to be an actor. The movie had opened right around the time I was in *The Normal Heart*. I took myself to an afternoon showing at the Sutton Theater, on East 57th. In the empty theater, watching my daughter's one wonderful scene, in which she becomes hysterical on a blind date gone wrong, I thought, *She can do this.* This was right before the major success she would have with *Ferris Bueller's Day Off* and then, of course, her iconic role in *Dirty Dancing*, but I knew there was no stopping her. She was too good—and I loved that.

I know that my father would have felt the same way if he could have seen me in *The Normal Heart*. Dad passed away several months before I took the role. He had been on dialysis for several years before ultimately dying of renal failure, at the age of seventy-five, on April 30, 1985.

Throughout my life my father also never stopped being my dad. After we first moved to Los Angeles, he went to Canter's deli every Sunday morning while we were still asleep to pick up blintzes, lox, bagels, cream cheese, pickled herring, whitefish, and more. His weekly shopping sprees earned him the nickname "the Goodie Man." Years later, in fact, on my fiftieth birthday, the doorbell of my New York apartment rang and I found a gigantic basket all wrapped with ribbons. Inside were blintzes, lox, bagels, cream cheese, pickled herring, whitefish, and more; the note was signed, "The Goodie Man is everywhere."

I believe that if he had been alive, my father would have come to see me in *The Normal Heart* and that he would have gotten it and would have been proud. My mother, on the other hand, never came. I never expected her to. Through the play I was moving closer to a new place of acceptance and ease within myself. The fear and shame that had been such a big part of me was slowly falling away, and in its place came an empowering sense of solidarity and, yes, pride. What people thought about me became less and less important.

Alas, my mother never, ever got it. Over dinner at her favorite restaurant in LA, knowing better but wanting to give her and us one more chance, I said, "You know, Mom, now that I'm divorced, the next important person in my life might be a man."

Without missing a beat, she looked right at me with a smile and said, "Oh, no, dear, that's not you." Then she finished her glass of champagne and we never spoke about it again.

In my mid-sixties, I had come to a point in my life where I realized that passion of any kind is gold.

CHAPTER FIFTEEN

I met someone, a guy, in, of all places, the 1987 revival of *Cabaret*.

It happened at the meet-and-greet on the first day of rehearsal for the show, which was set to embark on a seven-month national tour before opening on Broadway at the Imperial. All of the usual suspects were there: the producers, the creative team, the cast, production people, and the concessions department, which sold souvenirs, programs, and CDs—and was headed by Eddie, who gave me *the look*. A big guy in his late thirties with curly, prematurely gray hair, he was handsome.

As if the freedom and excitement of the road weren't erotic enough, Eddie was aggressively romantic with me as we began an intense but secret relationship. I was flattered by the little love notes—one more creative than the next—that this beautiful, talented man wrote me all of the time.

The unexpected affair added a layer of upheaval to the already tumultuous experience of reviving this much-loved show, which over the past two decades had taken on mythic proportions. In the original,

I was far from the top of the marquee, but now I had star billing. I was the draw, and I was also twenty years older!

In this production, Harold Prince took up his original role as director as did Ron Fields with the choreography. Joe Masteroff adapted the script to make Cliff bisexual, as he was in the movie version, which most people now thought of as the official version. Alyson Reed played Sally; Gregg Edelman had the role of Cliff; the opera singer Regina Resnik was Fräulein Schneider; and Werner Klemperer played Herr Schultz. As the only member of the original cast, I had to live up to the reputation I had built for the character long ago. With the challenge of my age and the fact that the character was no longer a surprise, I needed my storied Emcee to be as daring and dark onstage as he'd been in the film seen by so many.

I drove myself, as usual, crazy trying to achieve that goal as we performed to sold-out shows night after night, week after week, city after city. There was a lot of anticipation, since this was the first time I reprised the role of the Emcee after the film. This was a theater event, and I was at the center of it.

Facing three sold-out shows in Hartford, Connecticut, I felt the beginnings of a cold. I should have taken a few days off, but I have always feared disappointing an audience. Well, by the third performance, my throat was in so much pain I could hardly bare it. We were scheduled to open in Philadelphia in two days, the last out-of-town engagement before New York, and something felt really, really wrong. This was not just a sore throat.

I was rushed upon my arrival in Philly to Dr. Robert Sataloff, a top throat specialist, who delivered the news that I had burst a blood vessel on my left vocal cord, and would need to spend two, maybe three weeks on vocal rest, not speaking a word to anyone. And the opening in Philadelphia was in two days. Just a little more pressure: Our Broadway run was set to begin in only three weeks.

Before going on the road, I had become fascinated with the *I Ching*, introduced to me by a close Buddhist friend. The *I Ching*, or *Book of*

Changes, is a 3,000-year-old Chinese text used for telling the future—like astrology or palm reading (only more philosophical and spiritual). Forbidden to speak, I sat in my hotel room in Philly, looking to the *I Ching* to answer questions about my very uncertain future. It was at least something I could do while keeping my mouth shut. Maybe there was something to that old Confucian magic, because while I was flipping through the pages my mind flashed to a news brief I had read in *Time* magazine about an opera singer, who, after losing his voice, still went on by miming it while someone else sang for him from the wings.

The next day, I discussed it with Hal. (I had a pad and pencil in hand at all times, since I could only communicate by writing.) The plan was that while my understudy sang from the box above stage left, I would lip-synch and act the role. Hal OK'd the plan, but it remained to be seen whether the audience would accept it. We never lied to the theatergoers; the program clearly stated what was happening. At the end of the show, I brought my understudy onstage, and we took a bow together. The audience loved it and gave us a standing ovation.

For the next three weeks my understudy and I were two halves of an Emcee, and not one person asked for his money back. I was grateful to be there and to have found a way to play the part and keep the audience in their seats. But it was also one of the hardest times of my life. I didn't know if my voice was ever going to come back, and what condition it would be in if it did. The actor's voice is his everything.

One week after seeing Dr. Sataloff, I went for a follow-up visit. The cord showed only slight improvement, and he was doubtful that I would be well enough to make the Broadway opening. I went into New York to meet with Galli, my singing teacher, who gave me some gentle exercises while I waited to get the OK from the good doctor. The cast and crew worried, some for their jobs, some for me, some for both. Lip-synching could never be a solution on Broadway. Then came our last performance in Philadelphia, a Sunday matinee. I got the go-ahead from Sataloff to sing and did the whole show without my understudy. The voice was there and ready—maybe—to open in New York.

That was the backdrop to my already anxious state of mind when at 8:20 P.M. on October 22, 1987, opening night of the show at the Imperial, the set jammed. In the original production, back in '66, stagehands would move the scenery behind closed curtains on stage wagons, using long push poles or just their hands. Technological advances over the passing decades meant that in the revival all the sets now moved mechanically. It was supposed to make the production smoother, more problem-free. With most of the audience members already seated, I didn't know what to do other than take my place for the opening. I stood there waiting for the go-ahead. That's when I heard one of the stagehands loudly whisper in the dark, "Does anybody have a hanger?"

I looked in the wings, and there I found Eddie. My beautiful, sweet Eddie. He was staring right back at me like he always did, his eyes smiling and kind; he thought I could do no wrong.

Ultimately, Eddie and I lasted longer than *Cabaret* on Broadway. The revival wasn't an unmitigated success. It did run for 261 performances, but the critics complained it didn't compare with the original. Life inevitably changes things. It had certainly changed me. The last time I played the Emcee, I was a married man with two children. Now I was in a full-on romance with a man.

As our relationship progressed, I introduced Eddie to many of my friends, who were supportive. But no matter how much time he spent with them, they always perceived Eddie as at best enigmatic and at worst standoffish. Whether he thought he was more interesting that way or was simply hiding something, he didn't reveal a lot of himself to others.

I didn't care what anyone else had to say. I was over the moon. In private, Eddie continued to be the same devoted, adoring man that I saw from the wings opening night of *Cabaret* on Broadway. To mark my birthday one year, he hand-bound an accordion book no bigger than an inch high and a half-inch wide. I was moved beyond words as I opened the muted, Japanese-print cover to find, in the tiny, perfect handwriting done by this six-footer, "Rare is true love; true friendship is still rarer." The Jean de La Fontaine quote was followed by contributions from Lord Bryon, Alexander Pope, Heinrich Heine, and others—all on the subject of love and friendship. The theme was apt. Ours was a terrific friendship with the added dimension of a powerful physical connection. With him so romantic and me so ready, our relationship seemed like something I had been moving toward for a long, long time.

Still, I recognized some truth in what my friends had said about him. Even with me, he never totally let his guard down. After we had been together for a few years, he still insisted on maintaining a private life separate from ours.

Ironically, Eddie was the one uncomfortable with the idea that someone might think he was gay. It was as if God had played a joke on me. Here was the closest I had ever come to a real commitment to another man, and the man I chose to be with had trouble accepting his own truth.

But the heart wants what it wants, and I was in his thrall. Like anyone else in love, I was willing to settle for the conditions that had been imposed upon it. Eddie might not have wanted to let the world know I was his lover, but I did—and the first step toward that was introducing him to my family.

While I was in LA for an extended period in 1992 during pilot season, still chasing after that same bluebird of happiness, I sent Eddie a ticket so we could spend time together on the West Coast. I missed him, but I also wanted Ron and his wife, Maddie, to meet him.

My brother and Maddie had built a wonderful life for themselves in California. Ronnie, now Ron, a business genius, provided an Ozzie and Harriet–style existence for their two boys, Randy and Todd. They went to private schools and played tennis every day on their private court before heading off to UCLA. And still they were wonderful kids. Maddie was the most consistent and loving mother and person I ever encountered. When Jo and I were splitting up, and I no longer had a place in LA, I stayed with them, and Maddie accompanied me way downtown to court every day for the divorce proceedings. She made me laugh about Jo's über-fierce lawyer, who acted in court like she wanted me dead. A first-rate cook and true balabusta, Maddie made me all of my favorite comfort foods.

It was a tribute to my nurturing sister-in-law and my brother that I told them about Eddie. "I think I'm ready to commit, whatever that entails," I shared with Maddie. This was a time when things were beginning to change. Forty years earlier, I would have risked arrest with such an admission. Marc Blitzstein, who wrote *The Threepenny Opera*, was murdered in 1964 in the West Indies for being gay. America was slowly starting to come out of a period when being gay was considered a death sentence. Revealing to a family member that I was in love with a man was nothing short of a miracle. My brother and his wife, always knowing who I was and very much wanting to meet Eddie, invited us out to Malibu for brunch.

With Eddie sitting next to me at their breakfast table, I was contented. Ronnie and Maddie liked Eddie very much. He charmed both of them, and they were thrilled with my happiness. That emotion, however, turned out to be extremely short-lived. On the way back to the house I had rented on Clinton Street in West Hollywood, he became very quiet. I asked him what was going on, and he said he needed some air. "What do you mean?" I asked, but I didn't get an answer. When we got back to the house, he said, "I'm sorry. I'm really not ready for this. I need to marry a woman." And he ran as fast as he could. And that was that.

While I was deeply wounded by Eddie's response to my attempts to draw him into my family, after time had passed and I was able to look at that relationship with some distance, I saw my part in the puzzle of what had happened. I had spent a lifetime of making up stories and giving people messages that weren't exactly true, so that my life wouldn't be ruined. He was another version of me, twenty years ago. Eddie's resistance was much too familiar. You can't just turn that off because

now society says it's OK—or because you are in love. I had come up
in a time when being gay was so far from being OK that the sensibility never completely left me. Choosing someone like Eddie was another defense against understanding who I was. The fact that he didn't
want to be out and open fed into my own damaged psyche, which had
just begun to take baby steps toward acceptance.

What I didn't understand after my breakup with Eddie, and not
until four years later, when I took on the role of Amos Hart in the 1996
revival of *Chicago*, was that while being closeted felt so necessary for
survival that it was hard to let go, its side effects were equally damag-
ing. To not be seen, that terrible way of living, is at the core of Amos's
character's psychology. " 'Cause you can look right through me, walk
right by me," he sings in his big musical number "Mr. Cellophane,"
"and never know I'm there."

I almost didn't take the part. I had attended opening night of the
original 1975 production, because I was interested, for obvious reasons,
in Bob Fosse's choreography and direction of the musical (in addition,
Kander and Ebb wrote the music and lyrics for it after *Cabaret*). I didn't
connect with the cynical and dark piece—and I hardly remembered
anything about the small part of Amos, a cuckolded auto mechanic
played by the fine actor Barney Martin, except to note that I found
the character to be sorry for himself. I didn't like *Chicago*, and I couldn't
stand Amos.

A few days after I told my agent to pass on the revival of *Chicago* for
the City Center *Encores!* series, Charlie Repole—the friend who I had
worked with a lot over the years including on the summer tour of *George
M!*—called. "Someone in the office was talking about you and how
you turned down *Chicago*," he said. "You're wrong! You could score with
Amos. The part's a classic." He was adamant that I reread the script,
listen to the song again, and think about how I might approach the
role in a fresh way.

That's when it struck me that Amos had a peculiar dignity that I
was drawn to. Ideally, a role reflects some part of an actor's psyche. It

is a positive way of expressing and possibly exorcising those demons for the actor and audience. Throughout *Chicago*, Amos is mocked by the rest of the characters—particularly his wife, Roxy, who spends the play cheating on him and calls him that "scummy, crummy dummy hubby of mine." And yet he's the one guy whose actions are generous and genuine. He's the only one who seems to know what love really means.

I wouldn't play Amos as a loser. A man with the courage to love fully, no matter what people think of him, is a hero. At least to someone like me who had spent so much of my life fearing what loving unconditionally in my way would mean to others. With that in mind, I said yes and flew to New York two days later.

Our revival of *Chicago*, stripped of all the excess and cynicism of the original, turned out to be a huge hit. Ann Reinking—who had started out her career in the chorus of a Bob Fosse show before becoming a star and his love—played Amos's wife, Roxie Hart (a part she had taken over for Fosse's wife, Gwen Verdon, in the original) and choreographed the show "in the style of Bob Fosse." Bebe Neuwirth was brilliantly cast as Velma Kelly, the nightclub singer charged with murder, and James Naughton as her lawyer, Billy Flynn. The result was a great year in a show that would become the second-longest-running show in Broadway history, with more than 7,300 performances.

I felt deeply gratified by the show's success, as if it were a reward for having believed in and given all of oneself over in the way that Amos does. It was ironic, but I felt more open now than I ever had been as a young man. The experience that only comes with age made some of the old fears not disappear completely but at least recede. I was ready for adventure, which is exactly what I got when I received a call out of the blue.

"Joel Grey?" said someone in a tiny and strange but lilting voice.

"Yes."

"This is Björk."

I didn't know exactly what to say.

"Oh, hello. How are you?"

"I'm fine," said the Icelandic pop star. "I'm calling because I'm wanting to tell you that I want very much for you to be in a movie I'm making with Lars von Trier. We are shooting in Sweden right now. And we will try to send you the music for the number. But we are very happy if you are coming."

Then she hung up.

It was like getting a casting call from a woodland elf. But to work with Lars von Trier I would have accepted the job from one of the seven dwarfs. I thought his movie *Breaking the Waves* was one of the greatest films ever made and gladly accepted the role in his musical, *Dancer in the Dark*, of a former musical-comedy star from Czechoslovakia. No script necessary.

So in 1998, I flew to Stockholm, where someone from the studio picked me up to drive me to the hamlet where everybody was working on the film. I was put up in what I imagined was the only hotel in town. It was a little inn where the other cast members, such as David Morse, stayed, as well as tourists who had come to enjoy rural Sweden. I went out to dinner with Catherine Deneuve, one of the film's stars, and Lars von Trier. That alone was worth making the movie.

I still had little idea what I was doing in the movie. Although filmed in Scandinavia, it is set in 1960s Washington State, where Björk's character, Selma, a poor Czech immigrant, struggles to survive as she raises a son and slowly goes blind. Her rich fantasy life expresses itself in musical numbers filmed using more than a hundred small digital video cameras. That's where my character—Oldrich Novy, a former Czech movie-musical comedy star whom Björk's character worships and believes is her father—appears.

I remained in the small country village inn waiting to be called to set, but no call came. A day passed, then two, then three. Just when I was starting to really be nervous I received a call in my room from Lars: "We're recording your number."

Excuse me? Pardon me?

I was confused. I took for granted that we would record the music in a professional recording studio later in Stockholm—just as we had done for *Cabaret*. "We're recording," Lars said. "In room 176." That was not exactly the truth. We actually recorded our number "In the Musicals" in the room's eight-by-ten-foot bathroom. As if the song, with its Björkian off-kilter beats and chords, weren't strange enough. With one foot in the shower stall to improve the sound quality, I sang, "I don't mind it at all / If you're having a ball / This is your musical / I'll always be there to catch you." Björk, also performing, stood right in front of me holding on to the shower door to steady herself while she sang, "You were always there to catch me when I'd fall." Lars was lying on the bed, listening.

I had just taped a musical number for a major motion picture in the bathroom. Who would have ever thought? Maybe the younger me would have been put off by the lack of decorum, that this wasn't the right way to do things and so shouldn't be done at all. When you have to work so hard to keep a secret, you can't help but close off more parts of yourself than intended. No matter what anyone thought of *Dancer in the Dark*, I was just happy to be part of a project that was brave and independent. In my mid-sixties, I had come to a point in my life where I realized that passion of any kind is gold.

That is the power of a great work of theater—to help people find their way and to create new types of normal.

CODA

It was my brother who called on August 9, 2004, to tell me that Mother was gone. Her girlfriends had been expecting her for their weekly mah-jongg game that afternoon, but when she didn't show up, they were sufficiently alarmed that they called Ron. She was, after all, ninety-two years old. The police accompanied him to her apartment, where they found her, dressed to the nines per usual, lying on her bed, hands neatly folded, looking perfectly at peace. It was as if, feeling faint, she had decided to lie down for a minute, and that was that.

Ron—who had so much trouble forgiving our mother for always making him feel less than, especially less than me—told me that he planned to get rid of everything in her apartment. Right away. Tomorrow. Being a take-charge kind of guy, he was ready to dispose of her clothes, her photos, and even her artwork. (Mom had made something of a name for herself in LA as an artist, opening her own gallery called, what else, Grace. She made charming stylized paintings of children, but her most popular works were wooden, painted sculptures of children in the shape of chairs, which she called "chair people.")

In recent years, Ron and Mother didn't have a lot of contact, even though they lived around the corner from each other in LA. I told him that I was flying out tomorrow and that we would figure out what to do with the stuff that remained of her life. I couldn't let go as easily. As complicated a woman as she was and as complicated as our relationship had been, she was my mother, the woman who instilled in me my sense of beauty and creativity—in addition to the shame I felt for who I was. Up until the day she died, Mother never accepted that I was gay.

After Ron and I went through Mom's things and gave them to the grandchildren and friends, and I had returned home to New York, he called me to say he had found a diary she kept and asked if I wanted it. Of course I did. I always wanted to know more of her, in the hope of understanding what was behind her anger toward me. So Ron sent it to me in New York, and I opened it to the first page. I could quickly see her full venom across the page. After closing it fast, I handed the diary to my analyst at my next session where I asked her, "Do you think I should read it? Is there something for me to learn?" A week later, she advised me to throw it away, which I did without reading another word. I, who could never keep myself from reading reviews of my performances by strangers no matter how much they upset me, threw out my own mother's review. Who says we can't change?

It was a lot easier for me to be open about my sexuality: My mother and father were gone, Jo and I were divorced, my children were accepting of my truth, I had a group of loving, supportive friends, and the world was a much more open place in which to live. Still, when I agreed to play out various homoerotic themes in front of Duane Michals's camera for a book he was doing on the famous homosexual poet C. P. Cavafy, I worried I would be too anxious or inhibited to play the infamous poet.

I had met Duane—a remarkable photographer who has applied his cinematic, narrative style to many themes, including those involving gay culture—when he shot me as the Emcee for *Glamour* magazine in 1966. Over the years, he photographed me for various other magazines and became a valued friend. He was one of the few people I could talk to about gay stuff. He got it completely and was always a safe place to go.

He was definitely the only one who could have gotten me to play C. P. Cavafy in a large monograph that paid homage to the greatest Greek poet of the twentieth century. Duane imagined and staged elaborate scenarios, with various models and me as the poet (Duane always said I looked like him), that illustrated poems and essays that were overtly homosexual—like Cavafy himself.

After his shower he dried himself very carefully. And although he would never admit it, it had all been for my benefit.

The shoots, in tousled beds and outdoor cafés, were exciting for me, because the project was all about a desire that I hadn't been allowed to explore in my real life.

But here, at seventy-five years old, in front of Duane's elegant lens, I had a chance to act out those different vignettes that had played so many times in my own head. In one series, a young man sits at a café on the corner of Bleecker and Christopher streets where I, as Cavafy, spot him through the window. Emboldened by the young man's beauty, I follow him when he exits the café and as he walks down Christopher Street. The exhilaration of the moment was compounded by the fact that I hadn't met the model before the shoot, so it truly unfolded like an encounter between strangers.

The young man never looks back. Finally, he turns left, leaving Cavafy standing on a street corner, completely alone. In the next image, though, where we had just seen the boy exit, a hand appears. The young man has known all along that he was being followed. It is just an erotic game, and then they kiss. The kiss wasn't in Duane's original plan. The young man and I were just supposed to give each other a meaningful look. But I impulsively kissed him, on a public street not far from where I live and am known in the West Village, and the moment ended up in Duane's masterly book, because it perfectly encapsulated the unplanned yet inevitable.

The Adventures of Constantine Cavafy, published in 2007, was another step in my revealing myself to the world—an artful coming out much the way *The Normal Heart* had been. At the opening at Pace/MacGill, the top New York gallery for photography, the prints were hung beautifully. Even though I faced images in which I would have never allowed myself to appear in the past—a large photograph of me pouring oil for a massage onto my hands just above a naked man's butt—I felt comfortable as I milled about, as I would have at any other opening. I found Duane's art very special and was proud of our collaboration. Looking at the black-and-white prints, I came to understand my commonality with this aspect of Cavafy.

The gallery filled up quickly, and although the event was just beginning the place was already packed. Standing near the entrance, I spotted in the crowd a New York socialite I had known personally for years. She walked toward the elevator and pushed the button to call it. Having seen this longtime friend of mine arrive only a few moments earlier, I assumed her quick exit meant that perhaps she didn't feel well (when you get older, any out-of-the-ordinary behavior is a cause for concern about someone's health). I went over to the elevator and said, "Sorry I didn't get a chance to talk to you. Why are you leaving so early?"

She looked at me coolly and said, "I can't for the life of me understand why you would do such a thing."

It hadn't occurred to me that in this day and age, in a city known for its sophistication, in an art gallery, among friends, someone would criticize me simply for who I was. It was another variation of the same old thing I had heard my whole life, the thing my mother had put so succinctly by saying, "Oh, no, dear, *that's* not you."

I don't blame the woman at the gallery, or my mother, for having trouble accepting my story; it's taken me a lifetime to understand and accept my own particular set of contradictions.

For sure, a great deal of them lie within the realm of my sexual history. Even though my true powerful pull to intimacy is with men, the love of my life was unquestionably Jo Wilder.

That's quite something, since after our yearlong divorce proceedings, during which we communicated only primarily unpleasant things through our lawyers, we didn't speak to each other for a very long time. There were such hard feelings all over the place. Jo remained in LA, which she has made her permanent home, and I stayed in New York, which is mine. We lived completely separate lives with the kids as our only point of connection. Over time, our intermittent conversations about James and Jennifer turned into something of a friendship, albeit a distant one.

Despite the way things ended up between us, I can say unequivocally that the years I shared with Jo—loving, making a family, taking care of each other and our children—were my happiest. It was the realization of a lifelong dream. In the section of my junior high school yearbook where graduating eighth graders write their future aspirations, usually pro football player or astronaut, I wrote, "to be happily married."

When I eventually recovered from the divorce, I assumed I would find a similar connection with a man. But that hasn't happened. I turned out to be a much better family man than a gay man. I didn't know, and I still haven't figured out how to be that.

For the majority of my life I did everything I could not to feel that "shameful" thing, and when I left the straight world I still possessed the same instincts I had cultivated all those years before. I had powerfully pushed the idea down for so long that when I eventually tried to live in that world, I wasn't very good at it. I could never seem to let go of that feeling of shame or stop looking over my shoulder, even if I knew no one was coming to get me. That is simply the result of the time I came up in.

So it was no small achievement when, only recently, I actually said, to myself, those five little incredibly complicated words: *I am a gay man.*

It happened during an ordinary dialogue with myself, an un-momentous moment. I had left the gym and was walking down West 23rd Street. The day was beautiful, blue skies sharp against the red brick of Chelsea's historic townhouses. Hyperaware of everything around me, I thought, *The world today is not the world I was born into.* It was no longer criminal for men to love men, as it was for me at fifteen. Now gay men and lesbians could even get married. Rick—my longtime stage manager, one of the first people to make no bones to me about being gay, the one who had lost his lover, David, to AIDS while we were on tour—had recently married his boyfriend in Hawaii. Who in the fifties would have imagined it possible?

I didn't say it to anyone else but me. *This is who I am—I belong to a culture. I want to include myself in this world, whether I am in a relationship or not.* For the first time I was no longer judging the core of who I am, which is gay. I had not honored it before because what was so innately me was spoiled by my early life experience. Now I was ready to honor who I was and all those who suffered so that people like us could have a sense of freedom, love, and acceptance.

If you don't tell the whole truth about yourself, life is a ridiculous exercise. It's been a long struggle for me to internalize something that I have been working on since the Cleveland Play House, that the fundamental job of the actor is to tell about the human condition, to be a voice for the truest ideas and deepest emotions. Sometimes they are big ones, such as the nature of death in *On Borrowed Time*, the powerful material that informed the rest of my life. Or they are painful, such as in *The Normal Heart*, where I first talked to the world as a gay man. They are also lighthearted, such as *Wicked*, the 2003 musical in which I originated the role of the Wizard, and just plain hilarious, such as the stage madness in the 2011 revival of Cole Porter's *Anything Goes*.

No matter the subject matter, it is through the creative process that I am able to reinvent and make sense of the world around me. And often times I am the one who is changed. That is the power of a great work of theater—to help people find their way and to create new types of normal.

When *Cabaret* first appeared on Broadway, its themes of fluid sexuality, soulless survival, and easy violence were shocking and strange. But as Sally Bowles and the Emcee seeped into the public consciousness they changed the zeitgeist and the norms of what is appropriate. The stylized decadence of the Kit Kat Klub set trends and gave permission to those who wished to explore. The genius of *Cabaret* is that the audience can participate in the prurient appeal of Weimar Germany without getting their hands dirty. So what began as over-the-top and scandalous—Sally's fishnets and green "divine decadence" nail polish and the Emcee's crimson lips, rouged cheeks, and fake eyelashes—became cultural touchstones.

Having played all over the world, *Cabaret* is now an international touchstone. I remember traveling to Amsterdam in the '70s for the opening of the Dutch production, and with a free morning I was walking along the canals when I heard a tapping sound on a window. Through the glass, I could see a woman waving for me to come closer and I just assumed it was one of the city's many prostitutes. *Thank you but no thank you!* I continued walking, but the tapping grew louder until finally the woman threw open her window and yelled, "Joel Grey!" Turning around and walking back toward her in resignation, I geared up for the encounter since she was obviously not to be denied.

When I got in front of the canal house, the woman was no longer in the window. Before I knew it, she was coming out the front door. Only then, when she extended a large hand with green nail polish did I realize she wasn't in fact a woman at all. "I'm Sally Bowles," she introduced herself. Smiling to myself, I thought, *Of course you are.*

"How are you liking Amsterdam?" she asked.

"Very, very nice, thank you. Lovely to meet you."

What about finding Sally as a transvestite in the middle of the

Netherlands? That is simply the miracle of performance and of discovery. I was truly glad to meet her, and that she was free to be who she was. As Cavafy wrote in his poem "I've Brought to Art":

> Let me submit to Art:
> Art knows how to shape forms of Beauty,
> almost imperceptibly completing life,
> blending impressions, blending day with day.

My confidence in the search continues to grow, as does the authenticity of my existence now that the old attitudes and intolerance don't hold the same power to sting or stop the search. I am heartened by the irrepressible nature of desire, and that the fear of aloneness is greatly diminished by the inner quest that is now my companion. I know firsthand the power of transformation, that things can, and things do change. A doting mother turns into an antagonist; a wife becomes a stranger; children grow into adults; a husband of a woman finds he loves men; and the horror of a crass vaudevillian becomes the beautiful part of a lifetime.

Through it all the pursuit of art has always been a great friend, a place I could go when real life was too brutal or confining. Mastery can be pleasurable. But I think my Grandma Fanny summed it up best years ago when she was interviewed for a television special (along with my entire family, even The Sisters) right after *Cabaret* became a hit. "What is Joel Grey really like?" the host asked my grandmother, the last family member to be interviewed. Sitting under the bright lights with her makeup and hair done, this woman who never really learned how to read or speak English, all of a sudden became a TV star.

"You vanna know about Joel?" she said. "Joel vas de best!"

Although I was standing right there, it was as if she were eulogizing me.

"He used to come to my houz every Sunday for brawnch. I vood hev lox and bagels and crim cheez and pot cheez and barley soup and udder goodeez. And I vood say to everybody, 'Today iz Joel Grey's day. He should sing and dance and do anyting his heart desires.'"

Well, I'm still singing (in the same key), still dancing (but slower), and, finally, getting a lot of my heart's desire.

ACKNOWLEDGMENTS

There have been so many people on and at my side for as long as I can remember—of course, most dearly, my dad, mom, my daughter Jennifer, her husband Clark Gregg, granddaughter Stella, my son James, brother Ron, his wonderful late wife Maddie, my "cuzzin" Lee, Jo Wilder, and my godmother Jeanne Schneider.

I've had a long and lucky career, and I want to acknowledge all the creative people it's been such an honor to work with: the playwrights; composers and lyricists; directors; choreographers; set, costume, and lighting designers; producers—and all the brave and gifted actors I got to share so many stages with.

Thanks to David Kuhn and Becky Sweren for taking my book proposal (thank you, Emily Loose) to Colin Dickerman, who was an excellent, smart, and patient guide.

Thanks to the fine Rebecca Paley, who was kind enough to join me in the writing and kept me on track, with my eye on the long view. Also at Flatiron Books, Publisher Bob Miller, Publicity Director Marlena Bittner, and Associate Editor James Melia, for his charming persistence!

And thank you to Michelle McMillian for designing such a beautiful book.

I must call out on a personal level my longtime agent and most excellent friend, Gary Gersh.

Thanks, too, to my PR posse: Rick Miramontez, Molly Barnett, and Andy Snyder. And my private and personal posse: Nellie Johnson, Heather Girardi, Steve Chazaro, Steven Ferezy, and certainly not least, a slew of loving pals—lucky for me, too many to possibly mention here.

PHOTOGRAPHIC AND ILLUSTRATIVE CREDITS

ENDPAPERS

Front (The Musicals)

Cabaret (1966) © Friedman-Abeles, The New York Public Library for the Performing Arts

George M! (1969) © Friedman-Abeles, The New York Public Library for the Performing Arts

The Grand Tour (1979) © Roger Greenwalt

Chicago (1996) © Dan Chavkin

Wicked (2003) © Joan Marcus

Anything Goes (2011) © Sara Krulwich, *The New York Times*

Back (The Films)

Man on a Swing (1974) © Paramount Pictures

The Seven-Percent Solution (1976) © Alan Pappe

Buffalo Bill and the Indians (1976) © Joyce Rudolph

Remo Williams (1985) © Joyce Rudolph

Kafka (1991) © Alan Pappe

Dancer in the Dark (2001) © Canal+Film Four

PHOTOGRAPHIC INSERT

Cabaret (1966) © Friedman-Abeles, The New York Public Library for the Performing Arts

George M! (1969) © Friedman-Abeles, The New York Public Library for the Performing Arts

The Muppet Show (1976) © The Jim Henson Company

With Rock Hudson in Rome (1961) © Leo Fuchs

With James Garner on the set of *Maverick* (1959) © Warner Bros. Television

With the cast of *The Normal Heart* (2010) © Bruce Glikas

With Jennifer Grey at the Tony Awards (2015) © Mike Coppola/ Getty Images for Tony Awards Productions

With Idina Menzel in *Wicked* (2003) © Joan Marcus

CHAPTER-OPENING IMAGES

Chapter 11: courtesy of Lord Snowdon

Epilogue: courtesy of William Obrano

THROUGHOUT

"Joel Grey in Cabaret" by Al Hirschfeld © Al Hirschfeld Foundation

All other photos courtesy of Joel Grey.